Lord Krishna: The Best Project Manager

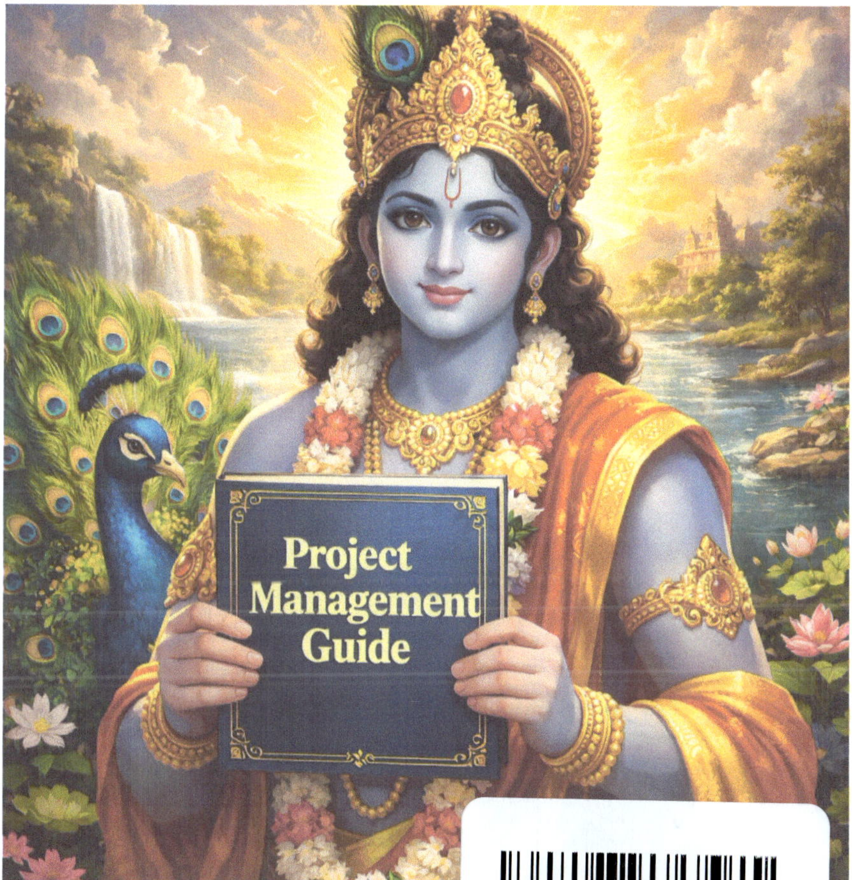

Pankaj Balooni

Printed in India

IndiePress

ISBN: 978-93-7197-245-1

First Printing, 2026

IndiePress

A division of Nasadiya Technologies Private Ltd.

Koramangala, Bengaluru

Karnataka-560029

http://indiepress.in/

Edited by MAP Systems, Bengaluru

Typeset by MAP Systems, Bengaluru

Book Cover designed by PH Keerthipriya

Publishing Consultant: Priyanshu Sarangi

Contents

Note to Readers

Dear Readers,

I've written this book in the way I understand things best—using bullet points and clear sections instead of long, continuous text. Over the course of my professional career, my mind has become more attuned to grasping information presented in this format. I've developed a habit of understanding concepts more clearly when they are laid out as short, crisp points—much like how ideas are shared in PowerPoint slides—so I chose the same approach here to make the teachings easier to follow and reflect on.

The reflections and interpretations of the *Shrimad Bhagavad Gita* in this book are entirely my own.

They represent the lessons I gathered while trying to understand this timeless scripture, especially through my experiences as a project manager. Over the years, I have faced moments of uncertainty, ambiguity and high-pressure decision-making during major project planning, programme execution and complex organisational transformations. In those moments, I often turned to Lord Krishna's teachings for clarity, guidance and calm. Over time, I realised that the wisdom of the *Shrimad Bhagavad Gita* offers practical lessons not only for life but also for navigating the dynamic and challenging world of modern project management.

In writing this book, I have also sought to connect the verses and teachings of the *Shrimad Bhagavad Gita* with the principles outlined in the PMBOK® Guide – 7th Edition. Doing so helped me see how timeless Krishna's wisdom truly is. While the PMBOK Guide focuses on principles, value delivery and adaptability—which I find especially relevant in today's evolving project landscape—the *Gita* offers insights that transcend time. By mapping these teachings to modern project management frameworks, I hope to demonstrate that the guidance Krishna gave Arjun centuries ago can still help us manage complexity, uncertainty and interconnected challenges in our projects and teams today.

I humbly acknowledge that every reader may interpret the same verse differently—and that is both natural and beautiful. Just as each person worships God for their own reasons, everyone may derive a unique meaning from the *Shrimad Bhagavad Gita*. My intention is simply to share what personally resonated with me and how these lessons helped me make better decisions, lead teams with empathy and maintain balance and focus through both professional and personal challenges. These reflections are not scholarly analyses or definitive interpretations; they are my personal insights—lessons I learned while navigating real-life situations where clarity and guidance were essential.

I hope you will read this book with an open mind and heart, seeing it as one perspective among many. My sincere wish is that these reflections offer you insights, encouragement or inspiration that can support you on your own journey—whether in your work, personal life or spiritual growth.

Above all, I pray that this book serves as a source of wisdom and clarity. May the teachings of the *Shrimad Bhagavad Gita* guide you in facing challenges with composure, making thoughtful decisions and growing both personally and professionally. May Lord Krishna bless you with strength, balance and insight, and may you find your own path illuminated by the timeless wisdom of this sacred scripture.

Introduction

Shrimad Bhagavad Gita – 'The Words of God'

Every reader approaches the *Shrimad Bhagavad Gita* in a unique way, bringing their own life experiences, values and personal perspectives to its teachings. It is a scripture that transcends time, offering wisdom that is not limited to any single era or context. What one person may find inspiring, another may interpret differently, yet at its core, it provides guidance, clarity and insight to anyone seeking direction. Its lessons resonate in countless ways, helping individuals navigate challenges, make difficult decisions and grow both personally and professionally. The *Shrimad Bhagavad Gita's* power lies in its universality—it speaks to the human condition in a manner that is deeply personal yet universally applicable.

For me, the *Shrimad Bhagavad Gita* has been more than a spiritual text. Over the course of more than two decades in the IT industry, my professional journey has been shaped by experiences in business management, commercial management, service transition and project and programme management. I have held roles ranging from Project Manager and Program Manager to Portfolio Head and IT Transformation Director. Each of these positions brought its own unique set of challenges—managing complex projects, leading diverse global teams, overseeing organisational change and ensuring successful delivery of high-stakes initiatives. Through it all, the wisdom of Krishna, as conveyed in the *Shrimad Bhagavad Gita,* has offered both inspiration and practical guidance.

Krishna's guidance to Arjun, especially during moments of uncertainty and doubt, resonates strongly with the challenges I have faced in my own career. Each initiative demands careful planning, strategic decision-making, leadership, conflict resolution and adaptability. These professional experiences mirror, in many ways, the dilemmas faced by Arjun on the battlefield—the need to act decisively, remain focused on the larger objective and balance competing priorities while ensuring that outcomes are achieved with integrity and purpose.

In my professional life, I have often encountered moments that tested my resilience and judgement. Decisions had to be made under tight timelines, sometimes with incomplete information and often with conflicting priorities across multiple stakeholders. In such moments, Krishna's teachings on clarity, duty and steadfastness have provided a mental framework for navigating uncertainty. The *Shrimad Bhagavad Gita* encourages reflection, discernment and deliberate action, which has been instrumental in shaping the way I approach challenges—whether it is negotiating with vendors, resolving team conflicts or ensuring that projects stay aligned with organisational objectives.

The book you hold in your hands is a reflection of this integration between ancient wisdom and modern professional practice. It is not an academic or exhaustive commentary on the *Shrimad Bhagavad Gita,* nor does it claim to provide definitive interpretations of its profound teachings. Rather, it is a personal account of how I have drawn lessons from the *Shrimad Bhagavad Gita* and applied them to my professional life. Having read and re-read the scripture multiple times, I have sought to extract practical insights that can guide project managers, team leaders and aspiring professionals in navigating complex environments. These are reflections shaped by lived experience, not theoretical reflections. I have applied these insights in real-world scenarios, and they have helped me make decisions that balance strategic goals, ethical considerations and human factors.

One of the most profound lessons I have drawn from the *Shrimad Bhagavad Gita* is the concept of ***dharma,*** or duty. Krishna's counsel to Arjun emphasises the importance of performing one's responsibilities with focus and dedication, even when circumstances seem challenging. In professional terms, this translates to taking ownership of projects and initiatives, staying committed to objectives and ensuring that the outcomes serve the greater good. In my career, this principle has guided me in moments where the easiest path may not have aligned with the organisation's or customer's best interests. It has reminded me to make choices rooted in long-term value rather than short-term convenience, to maintain integrity even when under pressure, and to lead by example for the teams I manage.

Leadership, as exemplified by Krishna, has been another cornerstone of my professional development. Krishna's ability to guide, inspire and mentor Arjun is a timeless example of how a leader can balance authority with empathy, strategy with compassion and decisiveness with patience. In my roles managing IT transformations, programme deliveries and multi-million-euro initiatives, I have encountered situations where clear guidance, encouragement and alignment with vision were critical. Krishna's approach emphasises that leadership is not about asserting power but about enabling others to achieve their best, fostering collaboration and creating an environment where the team can excel even under challenging conditions.

Equally relevant is the *Shrimad Bhagavad Gita*'s focus on clarity and decisive action. Arjun's initial hesitation and confusion mirror the doubts that often arise in complex projects. Krishna's guidance teaches that clarity of purpose, understanding the bigger picture and focusing on actionable steps are essential to overcome indecision. I have found these lessons invaluable when leading projects that involve multiple stakeholders, tight deadlines and high complexity. Whether negotiating timelines with vendors, aligning internal teams or resolving unexpected technical issues, the ability to step back, gain clarity and communicate direction has consistently proven to be the difference between success and stagnation.

The *Shrimad Bhagavad Gita* also highlights the importance of **ethical decision-making** and integrity, principles that are critical in any professional setting. Krishna consistently encourages Arjun to act righteously, balancing ambition and action with moral responsibility. In the corporate world, I have faced situations where the pressure to deliver results could tempt shortcuts or compromise ethical standards. Krishna's teachings have reinforced the idea that long-term success is inseparable from ethical conduct, and that true leadership requires making choices that uphold fairness, transparency and accountability, even when challenging.

Another lesson from Krishna that has influenced my professional journey is **adaptability and resilience.** Life in Gokul, with its unexpected challenges—from confronting demons to protecting the village from natural disasters—illustrates the need to respond thoughtfully and creatively to unforeseen circumstances. In IT project management, unexpected obstacles are the norm rather than the exception. System failures, delays in procurement, changes in regulatory requirements or last-minute stakeholder demands require adaptability. Krishna's approach reminds me to remain composed, assess options rationally and act decisively while keeping the ultimate objectives in mind.

The *Shrimad Bhagavad Gita*'s teachings on **focus and detachment** have also shaped my perspective. Krishna encourages action without attachment to outcomes, emphasising diligence and commitment while maintaining mental equilibrium. This does not mean indifference to results but rather cultivating a mindset where decisions are made with clarity and purpose, without being overwhelmed by fear, ego or anxiety. In professional practice, this mindset has allowed me to make balanced decisions, inspire confidence in my teams and maintain steady progress even in high-pressure situations.

Emotional intelligence, another key theme in the *Shrimad Bhagavad Gita,* is woven throughout Krishna's interactions with Arjun. The ability to sense, understand and respond appropriately to emotions— one's own and others'—is essential in project management. Managing diverse teams across geographies, negotiating with clients and vendors, and resolving conflicts require empathy, patience and strategic communication. Krishna's example demonstrates that emotional awareness, coupled with sound judgement, is central to guiding teams effectively and achieving collaborative success.

Throughout this book, I have endeavoured to highlight Krishna's project management wisdom through practical lenses—strategic planning, conflict resolution, ethical leadership, mentoring and emotional intelligence—illustrated with real-world professional examples. While I have not included specific project names here, readers will find that these examples show how the *Shrimad Bhagavad Gita's* principles can be applied in tangible, everyday professional contexts, from leading complex programmes to guiding teams through organisational change.

This reflection has been both a personal and professional journey. The *Shrimad Bhagavad Gita* has provided me with tools to navigate uncertainty, cultivate resilience, inspire collaboration and make decisions that balance purpose, ethics and pragmatism. It has shaped the way I view leadership, team management and project delivery, offering timeless guidance that continues to resonate across decades and continents.

Ultimately, the lessons of Krishna are not confined to the pages of scripture; they are living, breathing principles that can guide anyone in their personal or professional life. They offer a roadmap for leading with clarity, integrity and foresight, turning challenges into opportunities and creating meaningful impact. By sharing my journey of integrating these teachings into my professional practice, I hope this book inspires readers to reflect on their own approach to leadership, decision-making and life, discovering insights that are as relevant today as they were thousands of years ago.

The *Shrimad Bhagavad Gita,* through Krishna's guidance, demonstrates that success in any endeavour—be it spiritual, professional or personal—is not merely about achieving goals, but about the manner in which one acts, learns and leads. It teaches that the qualities of perseverance, clarity, ethical judgement and emotional intelligence are timeless and universally applicable. For me, the *Shrimad Bhagavad Gita* has been a compass, guiding decisions, shaping leadership style, and providing the strength to face challenges with courage and resilience.

In sharing this perspective, my intention is not to offer a scholarly treatise but a lived experience—how the wisdom of Krishna has informed, guided and transformed the way I navigate complex projects, lead teams and approach life. Through these reflections, I hope readers will see that the principles of the *Shrimad Bhagavad Gita* are not abstract concepts but practical tools, capable of shaping action, decisions and leadership in tangible ways.

Reading the *Shrimad Bhagavad Gita* with this lens transforms it into a guide for professional growth, self-leadership and meaningful impact. It reminds us that leadership is more than directing work—it is about serving others, guiding them with empathy, maintaining ethical standards and staying focused on the greater purpose. This book, therefore, serves as both a reflection of my professional journey and an invitation for readers to explore how Krishna's wisdom can illuminate their own path in work and life. The interpretations are supported by verses from the *Shrimad Bhagavad Gita,* as published by Gita Press, Gorakhpur, India.

Why I say Lord Krishna was the Best Project Manager

Lord Krishna, as depicted in the *Mahabharata,* embodies extraordinary leadership and project management skills. His ability to navigate complex situations, guide the Pandavas to victory in the Kurukshetra war, and uphold ethical principles makes him an unparalleled example of an effective project manager.

One of Krishna's most remarkable traits as a project manager was his strategic vision and meticulous planning. The Kurukshetra war was a massive undertaking involving numerous stakeholders, each with their own agendas, strengths and weaknesses. Krishna's first step in this monumental 'project' was to define the objective clearly: the restoration of *dharma.* Much like a modern project manager defining a project's scope and purpose, Krishna ensured that the Pandavas understood their ultimate goal and were fully aligned with it. His decision to take a non-combatant role—serving as Arjun's charioteer and advisor—reflects his strategic mindset. By positioning himself as a guide rather than a direct participant, Krishna demonstrated servant leadership, empowering his team while retaining the ability to steer them in the right direction.

Krishna's communication was a cornerstone of his success. He conveyed complex ideas clearly and inspired the Pandavas, especially Arjun, who was overwhelmed by doubt. Through his discourse in the *Shrimad Bhagavad Gita,* Krishna articulated a compelling vision and communicated it effectively, ensuring the team understood their roles, responsibilities and the greater purpose of their actions. This clarity kept the team motivated and focused on their goal despite overwhelming odds.

In terms of risk management, Krishna demonstrated exceptional foresight. He was always aware of potential dangers and challenges that could arise. He mitigated risks by preparing his team in advance, offering strategic advice and sometimes employing unconventional tactics to outmanoeuvre the opposition. His ability to anticipate threats and adapt strategies accordingly underscores the importance of risk management in complex projects.

When it came to negotiation, Krishna was unmatched. A prime example is his approach to peace talks with the Kauravas. He offered them peaceful solutions and tried to avoid war at all costs, highlighting his capacity for negotiation and conflict resolution. Even when his peace proposals were rejected, he maintained his composure and led his team without allowing the situation to deteriorate further. His diplomatic skills were essential for reducing unnecessary conflict and minimising potential setbacks.

Krishna's leadership style was multifaceted. He led by example, taking a non-combatant role yet holding immense influence over the course of events. His leadership was not about personal glory but about empowering his team—whether it was Arjun on the battlefield or the Pandavas in strategic planning. This exemplifies servant leadership, where Krishna's primary role was to serve his team's needs, guide them and enable their success.

In terms of problem-solving, Krishna exhibited an exceptional ability to analyse situations and propose solutions. Whether addressing Arjun's moral dilemma on the battlefield or finding ways to break deadlocks in the war, Krishna's solutions were innovative and insightful. He didn't simply provide answers; he challenged his team to think deeply, discover solutions themselves and develop a broader understanding of the bigger picture.

Delegation was another area where Krishna excelled. Despite being the ultimate strategist, he understood the importance of trusting his team with responsibilities. He delegated key tasks to Arjun, Bhima and others, allowing them to take ownership of their roles. His ability to trust his team while offering guidance when needed was crucial to the Pandavas' success. Krishna knew when to step back and when to intervene, ensuring that each team member could contribute meaningfully to the project's goals.

As a team builder, Krishna had an innate ability to bring out the best in individuals, creating a sense of unity and shared purpose among the Pandavas. Even in the most challenging situations, Krishna's vision kept the team focused, united and motivated. His guidance helped each member understand their value within the larger mission and contribute in ways that aligned with their strengths and capabilities.

Krishna's integrity was never in question. He consistently upheld *dharma,* always prioritising righteousness, truth and justice, even in the face of personal loss or difficulty. His actions were never driven by personal gain but always by a commitment to the greater good. This strong ethical foundation was the bedrock of his leadership, earning him the unwavering loyalty and respect of those around him.

Finally, Krishna's competence as a project manager was beyond comparison. His deep knowledge of warfare, governance and human nature allowed him to make informed decisions, adapt to new challenges and inspire others. His understanding of leadership, strategy and team dynamics made him the ultimate project manager—guiding the Pandavas to success while navigating the complex and ever-changing environment of the Kurukshetra war.

In conclusion, Lord Krishna's leadership in the *Mahabharata* offers a timeless model of project management. It demonstrates how effective communication, risk management, negotiation, leadership, problem-solving, delegation, team-building, integrity and competence can come together to lead a team to success—even in the most challenging and uncertain situations.

In today's boardrooms, data centres and various delivery projects or programmes, I have often found myself leaning on those same principles in my own career.

One particular project stands out. I was brought in to lead a large enterprise-wide technology implementation that was already in serious trouble. By the time I took over, the project was both delayed and over budget, with shaken client confidence and a team on the verge of burnout. It was clear there was no way to deliver early or magically reduce costs to bring it back within the original budget. Instead of dwelling on what had gone wrong, I focused on what could still go right—just as Krishna never wasted time regretting the past but concentrated on shaping the future.

My first step was to have honest, transparent conversations with senior management and the customer. Together, we agreed on a revised plan with **new, realistic timelines and a reset budget,** ensuring everyone was aligned and expectations were clearly defined. This moment of clarity shifted the tone of the project—panic was replaced with purpose.

Then came the human side of leadership: rebuilding trust and confidence within the team. Much like Krishna guiding Arjun through doubt, I reminded the team of the project's purpose and why their work mattered. I restructured delivery into smaller milestones, celebrated each success and created a sense of shared ownership. Slowly, frustration turned into momentum.

It wasn't an easy journey. Unexpected hurdles still appeared, and tough decisions had to be made. But with clear direction, renewed belief and strong collaboration, we delivered the project successfully—not within the original boundaries, but **within the newly agreed plan,** satisfying the client and restoring credibility.

That experience reinforced something Krishna teaches us repeatedly: leadership is not about controlling what has already happened; it's about guiding people through what comes next with purpose, courage and calm. The battlefield may now be a project boardroom instead of Kurukshetra, but the principles remain unchanged.

Leadership in Action: A Project Manager's Approach to Clarity and Guidance During Crisis

From a project management perspective, Lord Krishna's leadership during the revelation of his *Vishvarupa* (Universal Form) to Arjun exemplifies exceptional strategic insight, communication and stakeholder management. Throughout the *Shrimad Bhagavad Gita*, Krishna plays the dual role of project manager and mentor, guiding Arjun through the chaos of war, ethical dilemmas and personal crisis. However, it is in the moment when Krishna reveals his true divine form that his project management prowess becomes most apparent.

At this critical juncture, Krishna realises that to move Arjun past his doubts and fears, a deeper understanding of the bigger picture is required. Just as a project manager might unveil a key insight, dataset or visualisation to help the team grasp a complex problem, Krishna uses the revelation of his divine form to provide Arjun with the clarity he needs. This act serves as a strategic intervention, not only resolving Arjun's confusion but also ensuring alignment with the ultimate goal of the 'project'—the restoration of *dharma* and victory in the Kurukshetra war.

By revealing his true form, Krishna shifts Arjun's perception and helps him understand the broader context—one that transcends personal concerns, emotions and immediate outcomes. From a project management standpoint, this is a classic example of a leader stepping in to ensure the team understands the larger vision, the risks involved and the importance of moving forward with purpose. Krishna's actions here are akin to a project manager presenting a critical piece of information to align the team and reinforce commitment to the project's overarching objectives.

Furthermore, Krishna's approach highlights excellent stakeholder management. He recognises that Arjun's doubts are not merely about the tactics of war but about the deeper purpose and meaning behind the battle itself. By revealing his divine form, Krishna reassures Arjun of his role in the grand scheme, aligning his personal objectives with the greater organisational mission. Krishna's ability to deliver a clear and transformational message to Arjun—who is struggling with inner conflict—reflects an effective leadership skill in managing both team dynamics and stakeholder concerns, ensuring that individuals are fully committed to the mission.

Just as a project manager may need to help a team member understand the bigger picture, overcome uncertainty and gain clarity, Krishna's divine revelation serves as a leadership masterstroke that strengthens trust and commitment. It is a reminder that effective leadership can and should evolve—moving from tactical management to visionary guidance when individuals or teams need deeper purpose and alignment to achieve the ultimate objective.

One of the most challenging leadership moments in my career occurred during a **£3 million, four-month Data Centre IT Hall Readiness project**, delivering a fully operational **2,000 sq.ft. data centre hall** and IT managed services for a co-location facility. The project involved multiple teams—procurement, IT managed services, DC hosting, DCIM partners and the in-house DC build team—responsible for tasks such as **racks and hardware procurement, cabling, Telco/Meet Me Room readiness, Dark Fibre laying, last-mile connectivity, racking/stacking of devices and testing activities.**

Midway through the project, we faced a major crisis: **hardware procurement delays** and **last-mile connectivity issues** threatened the Go-Live date. Approval cycles in the procurement system were slow, vendor responses were lagging and Telco teams were struggling to coordinate installations for multiple connections simultaneously. Confusion was growing among teams, dependencies were misaligned and the risk of cascading delays could have derailed the project. Morale was low, and frustration was rising—much like Arjun's paralysis when faced with overwhelming uncertainty.

At that moment, I realised my role had to go beyond managing tasks. Like Krishna revealing his *Vishvarupa* to give Arjun perspective, I needed to **provide clarity, unify the teams and drive action across all stakeholders**.

Here's what I did and how it made a tangible difference:

1. **Sunrise Scrum Calls with Expanded Accountability**

    - I established **daily 'sunrise' scrum calls** including all team leads, vendors and **shipping/logistics agencies**, creating a single forum for visibility and accountability.

    - During these calls, we tracked **procurement requests, approval bottlenecks and shipping timelines**. Vendors and shipping agencies could see **how their delays cascaded across multiple workstreams**, which created urgency and ownership.

2. **Fast-Tracking Procurement**

    - I analysed the approval flow in the system and noticed unnecessary 'hop points' where requests moved across multiple tables and departments before reaching budget approval.

    - I redesigned the workflow: approvals were consolidated, the number of manual handoffs minimised and **budget issuance was automated wherever possible**.

- This significantly reduced the procurement cycle from weeks to days, allowing hardware to arrive **on time** and avoid impacting downstream installation schedules.

3. **Coordinating Last-Mile Connectivity**

- Telco terminations and Meet Me Room connections were critical path items but were often delayed due to lack of visibility on dependencies.
- I included **Telco vendors in the daily scrum calls**, walked them through the **entire end-to-end data centre timeline** and highlighted **how delays in their tasks affected Go-Live and other teams**.
- By creating transparency, clarifying priorities and aligning schedules, vendors expedited terminations, installations and testing by eliminating the bottlenecks.

4. **Visualising the End Goal**

- I mapped out the **complete operational data centre hall workflow**, showing how procurement, hardware setup, cabling and Telco connectivity all interlinked.
- Teams could see **how each activity influenced the critical path**, which turned the reactive fire-fighting into **proactive collaboration**.

Results:

- Procurement cycle times dropped significantly, allowing critical racks and hardware to arrive as per schedule.
- Last-mile connectivity issues were resolved quickly, preventing delays to Go-Live.

- Daily scrum calls improved cross-team communication and accountability, reducing dependency conflicts.
- The **data centre hall was delivered on time, fully operational and transitioned smoothly into BAU operations**.

Leadership during a crisis isn't about holding more meetings—it's about **taking targeted action that aligns stakeholders, removes bottlenecks and makes the bigger picture visible**. Just as Krishna revealed his *Vishvarupa* to give Arjun clarity and purpose, a project leader must intervene strategically, **showing the path forward while empowering the team to act decisively**. That combination of clarity and actionable guidance can turn potential failure into project success.

Mastering the Triple Constraint: Lord Krishna's Genius in Managing Cost, Time and Quality

Many times, Lord Krishna showed his exceptional ability to manage the triple constraint—cost, time and quality—in the *Mahabharata,* particularly during the Kurukshetra war. His strategic decisions and actions were not only aimed at achieving victory but also at optimising resources, reducing unnecessary losses and ensuring the war's swift progression while maintaining ethical standards. Krishna's foresight in balancing these critical factors allowed him to lead the Pandavas effectively, ensuring that the ultimate objectives were met with minimal costs and maximum efficiency. Let's delve into a couple of examples to understand it better.

Example 1 – The Planning and Execution of Bhishma's Fall

One of the most significant episodes where Krishna balances these constraints is the strategic plan to defeat Bhishma, the invincible commander of the Kaurava army. Bhishma was a formidable warrior, and his continued presence on the battlefield was causing heavy losses to the Pandavas (cost), prolonging the war (time) and threatening the quality of their strategy and morale.

Cost Management

Krishna understood that prolonging the battle against Bhishma would lead to significant losses—both in terms of soldiers and resources. To mitigate this cost, he devised a strategy that would require minimal force to achieve maximum impact. He suggested using Shikhandi, a warrior Bhishma had vowed not to fight (not as a shield, however). Both Shikhandi and Arjun fought with Bhishma at the same time. This tactic ensured that Bhishma could be neutralised without further unnecessary losses to the Pandava army.

Time Management

Krishna was acutely aware of the need to act swiftly to prevent the war from dragging on. The longer Bhishma remained on the battlefield, the more it would drain the Pandava forces and resources. By implementing a precise and targeted plan to incapacitate Bhishma, Krishna ensured that this critical phase of the war was resolved quickly, allowing the Pandavas to focus on other challenges.

Quality Management

Despite the urgency and resource constraints, Krishna did not compromise on the quality of the strategy. He ensured that the plan to defeat Bhishma aligned with the broader objective of upholding *dharma* and securing victory. By using Shikhandi, Krishna adhered to ethical boundaries while still leveraging Bhishma's vow against fighting women or those perceived as such. The quality of this strategic decision is evident in its effectiveness and minimal collateral damage.

Example 2 – Lord Krishna's Strategic Relocation: A Masterclass in Managing the Triple Constraint

Lord Krishna's decision to relocate his kingdom from Mathura to Dwarka offers a profound example of how to manage the triple constraint—cost, time and quality—effectively during a complex transition.

Cost Management:

The relocation of Krishna's kingdom was primarily motivated by the need for safety and security, especially after the increasing threats from Kamsa and other hostile forces. Krishna had to carefully manage the resources required for this transition.

- **Financial Resources:** Krishna ensured that the cost of building the new kingdom at Dwarka was carefully controlled. Dwarka was a strategic coastal city with the potential to facilitate trade, making it an economically viable option. Krishna did not simply abandon Mathura in haste but ensured that the resources required to establish a new, thriving kingdom were well-planned.
- **Human Resources:** Krishna wisely managed his army and subjects to ensure a smooth migration. His strategic leadership allowed for a successful transfer of not just people but also essential assets, such as treasures, artisans and skilled workers, without significant loss of productivity or morale.

Time Management:

The decision to move from Mathura to Dwarka was not a hasty one. Krishna understood the value of time, both in terms of personal security and long-term governance.

- **Timely Execution:** Krishna executed the move with careful planning. He didn't rush into the transition. The relocation of Mathura's people to Dwarka required significant foresight in organising transport, ensuring safety and establishing a new administrative structure at Dwarka—all of which needed to be carried out in a timely manner to prevent any lapse in governance or societal stability.
- **Strategic Timing:** Krishna understood that staying in Mathura while under constant threat would eventually lead to more harm than good. By acting at the right time, before the situation deteriorated, he ensured that

the move happened when the threat was imminent but not yet catastrophic, thus preventing loss of life or destruction.

Quality Management

While the logistics of moving an entire kingdom were critical, Krishna also focused on maintaining high standards of governance, culture and security in the new kingdom.

- **Maintaining Quality of Life:** Krishna ensured that the people of Mathura were not just relocated but given the opportunity to thrive in Dwarka. He built a fortified and prosperous city, ensuring that the quality of life for his citizens was high. Dwarka became a symbol of peace, prosperity and advanced urban planning, which can be seen as a long-term quality management strategy in leadership.

- **Ethical Governance:** Throughout this transition, Krishna maintained his commitment to *dharma* and ethical leadership. The move to Dwarka was not just a physical relocation but also a metaphorical one, where Krishna's leadership remained rooted in righteousness. He made sure that his governance in Dwarka was just and aligned with the values of truth, protection and prosperity for his people.

- **Security and Protection:** By choosing Dwarka, Krishna ensured that the kingdom would be well-defended against external threats. The city was surrounded by water and protected by a powerful fort, making it a place where both the people and their values could be preserved in peace.

My Experience: Mastering the Triple Constraint in a Multi-Million-Euro IT Carve-Out Programme

Just as Lord Krishna balanced cost, time and quality during the Kurukshetra war and the relocation to Dwarka, I faced a modern-day equivalent of that challenge while leading a multi-million-euro IT carve-out programme for one of the largest utility companies in the UK and Europe. The project's mission was monumental: to separate and rebuild the client's entire IT landscape from the ground up, creating a future-ready digital environment that was secure, scalable and operationally independent—all while adhering to strict timelines, budget constraints and enterprise-grade quality standards.

This was not just a project—it was a complete technological rebirth involving new infrastructure, modernisation, migration, compliance and operational transformation. Here's how I navigated the triple constraint:

Cost Management – Maximising Value Without Overspending

The project involved setting up entirely **new cloud and on-premises infrastructure**, building fresh contracts and licences, and procuring hardware and enterprise software. Managing costs across such a wide scope required precision:

- **Strategic Resource Allocation:** We designed and implemented a **VMware ESXi-based virtualisation platform** to host applications unsuitable for immediate cloud migration—a decision that avoided costly cloud refactoring and reduced short-term expenditure while keeping future scalability intact.
- **Smart Procurement and Licensing:** By consolidating software licences and leveraging vendor negotiations,

we kept capital expenses within approved limits without compromising functionality.

- **Optimised Cloud Utilisation:** Migrating SAP and non-SAP workloads to **Azure** was carefully phased, ensuring cost-effective use of compute and storage while avoiding idle resource charges.
- **Compliance Without Overspend:** Meeting **ISO 27001, ITIL and cybersecurity** standards was achieved by integrating essential controls like Splunk-based SIEM and IAM policies into existing systems instead of expensive third-party add-ons.

Result: The carve-out stayed within its **multi-million-euro budget envelope** while delivering a modern, future-proof IT estate.

Time Management – Delivering a Complex Transformation on Schedule

Time was our battlefield. The client faced strict regulatory and business deadlines—missing them was not an option. To ensure on-time delivery, we approached the programme like Krishna planning Bhishma's fall: focused, strategic and relentless.

- **Parallel Workstreams:** We ran **infrastructure setup, application modernisation and data segregation** streams concurrently, accelerating progress without compromising quality.
- **Structured Migration and Testing:** Application and data migration were executed in carefully sequenced waves, followed by **UAT cycles** and stakeholder sign-offs to ensure readiness without delays.

- **Accelerated Transition to BAU:** The **Target Operating Model (TOM)** and **Service Desk** were stood up early, allowing us to transition into steady-state operations immediately post-go-live.
- **Strategic Sequencing of Data Centre Exit:** Coordinating the exit plan with business continuity needs ensured we met the final milestone on time without disrupting critical services.

Result: The entire carve-out from new infrastructure design to full operational transition was completed **within the committed timeline**, despite its immense complexity.

Quality Management – No Compromise on Standards

While cost and time were critical, quality was the soul of this transformation. Like Krishna's relocation to Dwarka, where safety, governance and prosperity were non-negotiable, we held quality at the centre of every decision.

- **Enterprise-Grade Architecture:** We implemented **high-availability, low-latency infrastructure** across Azure and on-premises platforms, with built-in scalability and performance optimisation.
- **Robust Security and Compliance:** All environments were designed to meet **ISO 27001, ITIL and cybersecurity** standards, with security baked into every layer—from virtual networking and firewall rules to IAM and SIEM logging.
- **Seamless Integration:** Post-migration, we validated upstream and downstream integrations, patched and

hardened OS layers and documented SOPs to ensure stable, supportable operations.

- **Business Continuity and User Experience:** Transition to BAU operations was meticulously planned, ensuring end users experienced zero disruption while gaining enhanced reliability and performance.

Result: The final solution not only met but **exceeded client expectations** on stability, performance and security—creating a foundation that supports future growth and digital transformation.

Like Krishna's strategic brilliance on the battlefield and beyond, this carve-out programme succeeded because of meticulous balance. A **fully independent, secure and future-ready IT landscape** was delivered, meeting every cost, time and quality commitment—and enabling the client to move forward with confidence into their next chapter of digital evolution.

A Fusion of Ancient Wisdom and Modern Project Management

The **PMBOK® (P**roject **M**anagement **B**ody **of K**nowledge**) Guide – Seventh Edition**, introduced **twelve Project Management Principles** and **eight Project Performance Domains** to provide a more flexible, outcomes-driven approach to project management. This shift aligns better with the diverse methodologies used in modern project environments.

In my honest opinion, the seventh edition reflects today's evolving project management trends quite well, such as the increased use of agile and hybrid methodologies. It also includes technologies, strategies and market demands that were not addressed in earlier editions, in my opinion. Its main purpose is to make this guide more relevant and useful for today's project managers, so that they can understand modern work approaches and manage their projects efficiently. These updates ensure that the PMBOK guide is always up-to-date and keeps pace with the latest trends in the industry.

But, I feel that the modern ways of management we are using today are still based on ancient wisdom. Meaning, the foundation of the concepts and practices we use today is very old, and that wisdom is still applicable. These modern techniques, no matter how advanced, find their roots in ancient teachings. Therefore, this old wisdom is still relevant and can be quite useful for our projects.

Drawing on my extensive experience in project management and the sacred knowledge of *Shrimad Bhagavad Gita,* I have tried to map the knowledge areas of the PMBOK's seventh edition to the teachings of Lord Shri Krishna.

The various forms of Lord Krishna—such as a guide, planner, mentor and leader—are deeply connected to the principles of project management. By mapping their qualities, such as vision, adaptability, decision-making, stakeholder management and conflict resolution to the PMBOK's management principles and performance domains, I have tried to show how ancient knowledge can influence today's project leadership and success.

12 Project Management Principles on PMBOK

1. **Stewardship**

   - ***Verse:*** *'Karmanye vadhikaraste, ma phaleshu kadachana'* (2.47)
   - ***Meaning:*** 'You have the right to perform your prescribed duties but are not entitled to the fruits of your actions.'
   - ***Connection:*** In project management, stewardship is about taking full responsibility for guiding the project to its objectives, focusing on the actions and decisions within your control. Krishna told Arjun that his control lies in his action, in the drawing of the bow and releasing of the arrow, but not in whether the arrow hits the target. Similarly, a project manager can control the planning, execution and efforts of the team, but the outcome may be influenced by external factors beyond their control. Krishna's message teaches us to focus on doing our best with dedication and discipline, trusting that success comes through right action, not by obsessing over the results. Just as Arjun focuses on perfecting his aim and skill with the bow, a project manager focuses on executing tasks with excellence and clarity, without letting uncertainties or external challenges deter them from their responsibility. By focusing on the journey, the project manager can ensure steady progress while remaining detached from the unpredictability of the outcome, just like Arjun trusting his training and dedication, not worrying about the target's fate.

2. **Team Collaboration**

   - ***Verse:*** *'Yad yad acharati shreshthas, tat tad evetaro janah'* (3.21)

- ***Meaning:*** 'Whatever a leader does, others follow. Whatever standards they set, the world emulates.'
- ***Connection:*** Effective team collaboration starts with strong leadership. Krishna emphasises that leaders set the tone for the entire team through their actions, attitude and behaviour. Just as a leader's integrity, clarity and respect influence the team, their actions become a blueprint for how the team will collaborate. In project management, this means that the leader's behaviour, whether it's demonstrating open communication, accountability or respect, will be mirrored by the team. If the leader approaches the project with dedication, transparency and a solution-oriented mindset, the team is more likely to follow suit. Krishna's teaching shows that leadership by example is crucial in building a collaborative environment. When a leader leads with humility, respect and openness, it fosters an atmosphere where team members feel valued, encouraged to contribute their ideas and are motivated to work together towards common goals. Just as Arjun would follow Krishna's guidance in battle, the team will follow their leader's example, creating a cohesive and productive environment where collaboration thrives. This principle highlights that collaboration is not just about teamwork but about creating a culture of shared responsibility, trust and mutual respect from the top down.

3. **Stakeholder Engagement**

- ***Verse:*** *'Samatvam yoga uchyate'* (2.48)
- ***Meaning:*** 'Equanimity of mind is yoga.'

- ***Connection:*** Engaging stakeholders effectively requires emotional intelligence, balance and the ability to remain calm under pressure—all of which are qualities that Krishna emphasises in the *Shrimad Bhagavad Gita*. Krishna teaches Arjun that achieving equanimity, or a balanced state of mind, is essential for effective action. In the context of project management, this means that a project manager should approach stakeholder engagement with impartiality, maintaining a calm and balanced attitude when addressing different viewpoints, concerns and demands.

  Krishna's teachings on maintaining equanimity are exemplified when he advises Arjun to remain unaffected by the swings of emotion in difficult situations. In Chapter 2, verse 48, Krishna explains that true yoga is the ability to stay steady and clear-headed, whether in success or failure, gain or loss. Similarly, in stakeholder engagement, the project manager must approach each stakeholder with the same level of respect and emotional control, regardless of the emotional intensity or conflicting opinions.

  For example, imagine a project where different stakeholders have opposing views on a key decision. One stakeholder is overly optimistic and wants to push forward without proper analysis, while another is more cautious, fearing the risks. A project manager, following Krishna's principle of *samatvam* (equanimity), would listen to both sides calmly, analyse the situation impartially and bring both parties together to find a balanced solution that serves the project's goals. By maintaining emotional control and not being swayed by personal biases or stress, the project manager ensures productive conversations, builds trust and fosters collaboration, all while keeping the project on track and focused on the end goal.

Krishna's message is clear: as a leader, one should not be swayed by the emotional reactions of stakeholders but should remain focused on the higher purpose of the project. By engaging with stakeholders calmly, respectfully and with a balanced perspective, the project manager can create a harmonious and productive working relationship, even in the face of challenges. This mindset fosters cooperation, reduces conflict and ensures that the interests of all stakeholders are addressed in a fair and constructive manner.

4. **Value Delivery**

- ***Verse:*** *'Svadharme nidhanam shreyah, paradharmo bhayavahah'* (3.35)
- ***Meaning:*** 'It is better to perish in one's own duty than to thrive in another's.'
- ***Connection:*** In project management, delivering value is deeply tied to understanding and fulfilling one's own role and responsibilities. Krishna emphasises that each person should focus on their own *dharma* (duty), as it is through the execution of our unique roles that we contribute meaningfully to the larger purpose. A person who understands their daily deliverables and executes them with the utmost quality is in a position to create real value for the project. If a team member fulfills their role with dedication, they not only contribute to the success of the project but also grow in expertise and

responsibility, eventually adding more value as the project progresses.

For example, in a project, a team member assigned to a specific task—whether it's developing code, resolving an incident ticket, monitoring alerts, designing a user interface or managing a stakeholder relationship—must first understand the importance of their individual contributions. If they consistently deliver quality work, they build trust and reliability within the team. This, in turn, allows them to take on more complex tasks and add value in ways beyond their initial role. As Krishna advises, one must focus on one's own duties (*Svadharma*), rather than trying to perform someone else's work, which can lead to confusion, inefficiency and lack of quality.

In a well-functioning team, when each member fully understands their deliverables and executes them with quality, they contribute to the collective success of the project. This is where Krishna's principle of sticking to one's *dharma* plays a crucial role. If every team member works in alignment with their strengths, the project as a whole will be stronger, delivering greater value.

The project manager's role is also critical in recognising these strengths and ensuring that each team member is focused on their respective areas of expertise. By empowering individuals to take ownership of their roles, providing the necessary resources and ensuring alignment with the project's objectives, the manager facilitates an environment where value delivery is maximised. When each person performs their role with excellence, the project's overall quality improves and the outcome is more likely to meet or exceed expectations.

Krishna's message teaches that by staying true to one's own purpose and responsibilities, a person ensures that the quality of their work contributes to the overall success of the project. A project is not just about meeting deadlines but about achieving quality through collective effort, with every team member bringing their best to the table.

5. **Systems Thinking**

- ***Verse:*** *'Mamaivamsho jiva-loke, jiva-bhutah sanatanah'* (15.7)
- ***Meaning:*** 'All living beings are but fragments of my eternal self.'
- ***Connection:*** Krishna's verse highlights the interconnectedness of all beings in the universe, a concept that is directly applicable to project management through the lens of systems thinking. Just as every living being is a part of a larger, interdependent system, each element of a project—whether it's the team, tasks, resources or stakeholders—is part of a greater whole. Systems thinking encourages project managers to understand and appreciate these interconnections, recognising that decisions in one area of the project can have far-reaching consequences on other areas.

It can also be understood in the context of modern delivery approaches, where seemingly independent Agile sprints can exist as interconnected parts of a larger waterfall programme. While each sprint delivers incremental value and focuses on short-term goals, it ultimately contributes to the success of the overall project, which may follow a more structured and sequential approach. This layered view reflects the essence of systems thinking—individual components (like sprints, modules or workstreams) may appear self-contained, but they derive their purpose and direction from the broader system they belong to.

Just as Krishna teaches that all beings are fragments of a greater whole, each sprint, task or deliverable exists within a wider project ecosystem. Decisions made within one sprint can influence future stages, stakeholder expectations and even strategic outcomes. Recognising this interdependence allows project managers to align iterative work with long-term objectives, balancing agility with overarching structure. It reinforces that no part of a project operates in isolation; even Agile elements must integrate seamlessly into the larger delivery framework.

By adopting a systems thinking approach, a project manager can better understand the complexities of the ever-changing environment that projects operate in. The approach allows managers to recognise how external elements—such as market changes, stakeholder needs or technological advances—can influence the course of the project. This broad perspective is essential for anticipating challenges, managing risks and making decisions that align with the overall objectives of the project.

Moreover, systems thinking pushes projects to be more flexible and adaptable to unforeseen changes. Krishna's teachings remind us that nothing exists in isolation; everything is part of a larger system that is continuously evolving. Similarly, projects must remain agile and responsive to the changing dynamics around them, whether they come in the form of unexpected challenges or shifts in the external environment. By seeing the project as an interconnected system, a project manager can proactively adapt to changes, ensuring that the project stays on course even in the face of uncertainty.

This holistic understanding helps ensure that the project is not just focused on short-term gains but also on long-term sustainability. By viewing the project as a dynamic and interconnected whole, a project manager can make informed decisions that consider the broader impact of each action. Krishna's wisdom in this verse teaches us that all elements of a project are intrinsically linked, and recognising this interdependence allows project managers to navigate complexity, embrace flexibility and lead their teams towards successful outcomes, regardless of the challenges that arise.

6. **Leadership Behaviour**

- ***Verse:*** *'Na buddhi-bhedam janayed, ajñanam karma-sanginam'* (3.26)
- ***Meaning:*** "Don't confuse those who are focused on the results of their actions. Instead, motivate them by doing your own work with dedication.
- ***Connection:*** This verse emphasises the role of a leader who inspires their team not by forcing actions or confusing them with outcomes but by fulfilling their own duties with dedication and focus. Krishna

advocates for leading through example, performing one's responsibilities with clarity and purpose, thereby motivating others to do the same. A leader must exhibit calm, focused and ethical behaviour, showing their team the way to act with integrity and commitment.

While it is true that Krishna did pick up a weapon and fought in the Kurukshetra war—particularly in an intense battle between Arjun and Bhishma—it is important to understand the context of his actions. Krishna's role as a warrior in the war was symbolic of his commitment to *dharma* (righteousness). Although Krishna did not initially choose to fight in the war, he did intervene when it became absolutely necessary. For instance, in the fight against Bhishma, Krishna, who was Arjun's charioteer, took up the wheel of his chariot to fight Bhishma when Arjun was unable to defeat him. However, Krishna's involvement was not driven by personal desire or attachment to victory. Instead, it was rooted in his responsibility to uphold righteousness and protect *dharma,* demonstrating that a leader sometimes must take decisive action when the situation calls for it.

Krishna's leadership was defined not by his physical combat, but by his unwavering commitment to his duties. His action against Bhishma was an exception rather than the norm, showcasing that a leader must be prepared to step into situations that demand intervention for the greater good. His actions on the battlefield, whether in combat or as a guide, were all aimed at upholding righteousness, not personal gain or attachment to the outcome. This teaches that a true leader, while always focused on duty, may sometimes need to act decisively when circumstances demand it, ensuring the larger cause is upheld.

In the project management context, Krishna's approach reflects that leaders must guide their teams, sometimes making tough decisions, but always with clarity of purpose and never distracted by the outcome. They inspire through their commitment to the process, regardless of the external pressures or challenges they may face. Just as Krishna did not seek fame or reward from his actions but acted out of his duty, leaders should remain focused on their responsibilities, leading by example and ensuring the team stays aligned with the broader objectives.

7. **Tailoring**

- ***Verse:*** *'Chatur-varnyam maya srishtam, guna-karma-vibhagashah'* (4.13)
- ***Meaning:*** 'I have created the four divisions based on qualities and actions.'
- ***Connection:*** Krishna's creation of the four *varnas* (Brahmin, Kshatriya, Vaishyas and Shudra) emphasises the importance of assigning roles based on the inherent qualities and capabilities of individuals. This ensures that each group contributes in the most effective way to society, creating a balanced and harmonious system. Similarly, in any organisation or project, understanding the strengths and limitations of individuals and assigning them roles, accordingly, ensures that each team member is able to contribute their best.

Tailoring is not just about assigning the right roles to people, but also about adapting solutions to fit the specific needs of the situation. It recognises that no one-size-fits-all approach works, whether in team roles or when providing solutions to clients. Just as Krishna divided society into *varnas* based on qualities and actions, businesses must offer **custom-fit solutions** to their customers, taking into account their unique needs, constraints and goals. Tailoring involves creating solutions that are flexible, adaptable and personalised to suit the customer's requirements.

For example, in a project, the solution offered to a customer should not be generic; it should be designed with the customer's specific context in mind—whether it's their budget, timeline, technological infrastructure or unique challenges. By understanding and addressing these factors, a project manager or business leader can offer a solution that best fits the customer, ensuring the project's success and the customer's satisfaction.

Just as the four *varnas* in society complement each other, tailored solutions provided by an organisation must align with the customer's needs and the capabilities of the team to ensure that all parties work in harmony towards a common goal. Tailoring, therefore, is a comprehensive approach that extends beyond internal processes to include how we serve and fulfill the specific requirements of those we are working for, ensuring long-term success and value creation.

A perfect example of tailoring in my career was when I led the **deployment of CyberArk Privileged Access Management (PAM)** for a **major UK utility**

client—a project critical to their cybersecurity posture and regulatory compliance. The client's environment was complex: a mix of on-premises systems, legacy applications, cloud workloads, stringent compliance requirements and a zero-tolerance policy for downtime.

Delivering a 'standard' PAM implementation would have failed miserably here. Instead, we tailored every aspect of the project—from architecture to policies—around the client's unique context:

- **Customised Solution Architecture:** We designed and installed **CyberArk Core PAS components**—including Password Vault, Central Policy Manager (CPM), Privileged Session Manager (PSM) and Vault Web Access—with **high availability and low-latency** infrastructure. A **disaster recovery** setup was included to meet the client's uptime SLAs.
- **Tailored Integrations:** Rather than using default connectors, we **integrated CyberArk with Active Directory and LDAP**, tied monitoring alerts into **ServiceNow** for automated ticketing and connected with the client's **SIEM** for real-time alerting.
- **Client-Specific Policies:** Password rotation and access control policies were crafted based on the **least privilege principle** but adapted for the client's operational workflows, service account usage and compliance mandates.
- **Adapted Security Controls:** We deployed **Just-in-Time (JIT) access**, session isolation and session monitoring tailored to their internal risk posture and governance requirements.

- **Operational Fit:** Automated workflows were built for provisioning and de-provisioning accounts, reducing manual overhead and aligning with the client's ITIL-based operations model.
- **Context-Aware Vulnerability Management:** Beyond deployment, we conducted **bi-annual patching for approximately 500 servers**, running scans and penetration tests with **Qualys**. Where patches posed risks to application stability, we documented exceptions with mitigation steps—balancing security with operational performance.

This wasn't merely a deployment—it was **a bespoke security solution designed for their world**. Every decision—from architecture to policy—was shaped by their **business priorities, infrastructure realities, compliance landscape and operational model.**

The result? The client achieved a **robust privileged access framework**, improved audit readiness, enhanced compliance posture and significantly reduced the attack surface—all without disrupting business continuity.

Just as Krishna assigned roles based on individual qualities to create a balanced and efficient society, tailoring in project management means **molding our methods and solutions to the specific environment and objectives at hand.** It's not about abandoning structure—it's about intelligently adapting structure to fit reality. The CyberArk project's success was not due to rigid process adherence but because we *listened, understood and tailored*—ensuring the solution was not just technically sound, but contextually perfect.

8. Quality

- ***Verse:*** *'Yatah pravrittir bhutanam, yena sarvam idam tatam'* (18.46)
- ***Meaning:*** 'By performing one's natural occupation, one worships the Creator from whom all living entities have come into being and by whom the whole universe is pervaded. By such work, a person easily attains perfection.'
- ***Connection:*** Krishna emphasises the importance of performing one's duty with sincerity, dedication and focus, as this leads to mastery and perfection. When one engages wholeheartedly in their natural work, with devotion and commitment, they achieve not just external success but internal satisfaction and excellence. Krishna's message is that when we align our actions with our true purpose and perform them with mindfulness, the result will naturally be perfect and of high quality.

  In the context of project management, **quality** is not just about meeting the basic requirements but about a deep commitment to excellence in every aspect of the project. Quality stems from consistent effort, a keen eye for detail and a continuous desire to improve and refine processes. Just as Krishna advocates for devotion to one's duties, delivering high-quality outcomes in a project requires dedication and an ongoing focus on perfection in every task. It's the small, seemingly insignificant actions done with care and attention that cumulatively lead to a project that stands out in its excellence.

A notable example from the *Mahabharata* where Krishna emphasised the importance of quality in work can be seen when he guided **Arjun** during the **Kurukshetra War**. Krishna's guidance in the *Shrimad Bhagavad Gita* was not just about fulfilling duties, but about fulfilling them with integrity and focus on the highest possible standard. One of the key moments that illustrate Krishna's own emphasis on quality was when he advised **Arjun** not to rush his actions, but to focus on the precision of his aim and to execute his duties without distraction.

During the war, when Arjun was hesitant about killing his loved ones, Krishna reminded him that his responsibility was to fight in the battle and he should do so with commitment, focusing on the perfection of his craft as an archer. Krishna encouraged him to give his best effort, irrespective of the results. This is a lesson in the **quality of work**—to perform one's duty with full attention and dedication, without concern for the fruits, but with a focus on achieving the highest standard of work possible in the given circumstances.

Krishna himself also demonstrated quality in his actions, especially in the role of a **charioteer** to Arjun. Despite his divine status, Krishna took on this humble role and provided invaluable support to Arjun. He didn't take this role lightly, and his guidance and strategic advice were key to Arjun's success. In doing so, Krishna exemplified that no matter the role or task, it should be done with full commitment, excellence and a focus on perfection.

This emphasis on doing one's duty to the best of their ability is a powerful lesson for project managers today.

Ensuring that quality is maintained at every stage of a project, whether in planning, execution or delivery, is vital for achieving the best outcomes. By maintaining a focus on quality, much like Krishna emphasised in his teachings, we can ensure that our projects not only meet the basic goals but also exceed expectations, delivering exceptional value to all stakeholders.

9. **Complexity**

- ***Verse:*** *'Avyaktadini bhutani, vyaktamadhyani bharata'* (2.28)
- ***Meaning:*** 'All beings are unmanifest at their origin, manifest in their interim state and unmanifest again at their end.'

1. **Unmanifest Origin (Ambiguity at the Start):**

   Just like beings are 'unmanifest' at their origin, in projects, the initial stages often involve ambiguity. Goals, requirements and objectives may not be fully clear or tangible.

2. **Manifest Interim State (Interconnected Dynamics):**

   In the interim state, beings become manifest and interact dynamically, much like the execution phase of a project. During this phase, multiple moving parts interact, creating interdependencies and uncertainties.

3. **Unmanifest End (Uncertainty in Outcome):**

   At the end, beings return to an unmanifest state, signifying the uncertainty and potential lack of visibility about the outcomes or impacts of complex systems or projects.

- ***Connection:*** Addressing complexity requires a combination of structured tools (like RAID), a clear understanding of scope, a holistic perspective and principles like system thinking and strong leadership. Drawing wisdom from both modern frameworks and timeless teachings like *Shrimad Bhagavad Gita* equips project managers to navigate complexities with resilience and clarity.

  Krishna's verse serves as a reminder of the ***cyclical nature of projects:***

  Transient Nature: *Just as beings transition between unmanifest and manifest states, projects evolve through initiation, execution and closure, with complexities emerging at each phase.*

  Patience and Clarity: *Embrace uncertainties with composure, focusing on the ultimate objective.*

  Adaptability: *Acknowledge the fluidity of project circumstances, using a balanced and focused mindset to navigate through them.*

  In the PMBOK, **complexity** refers to characteristics of projects, programmes or systems involving ambiguity, uncertainty, interconnection of multiple elements and dynamic interactions over time. Building on this idea of interdependence, Krishna further explains the components behind all actions.

- ***Verse:*** *'Panchaitāni mahābāho, kāranāni nibodha me, sānkhyekritānte proktāni, siddhaye sarvakarmanām.'* (18.13-14)

- ***Meaning:*** 'Know, O mighty-armed Arjun, these five factors declared in the Sankhya system for the accomplishment of all actions.'
- ***Connection:*** This verse introduces the concept of the **five causes** necessary for the accomplishment of any task or action:

1. The body (*Adhishthana*)
2. The doer (*Karta*)
3. The various instruments (*Karana*)
4. The efforts or actions (*Cheshta*)
5. Divine will or destiny (*Daivam*)

Relating to Complexity in the PMBOK:

1. **Multiple Factors at Play:**

   Complexity often arises because a project or task involves multiple interdependent factors. This verse explains that no task can be accomplished by focusing on just one element alone—it's the interaction between various components that defines the outcome.

2. **Uncertainty and Divine Will:**

   In project management, there's always an element of uncertainty and factors beyond control (e.g., market forces, stakeholder decisions). This aligns with the concept of ***'Daivam'*** or destiny in the verse, signifying that not everything can be predicted or controlled.

3. **Interdependencies and Balance:**

   The interconnectedness of the 'body,' 'doer' and 'instruments' mirrors the interconnected nature of systems and processes in projects, highlighting the need to address and manage complexity effectively.

Continuing this theme of cycles and interdependence, Krishna further warns of the consequences of ignoring this natural flow.

- ***Verse:*** *'Evam pravartitam chakram nānuvartayatiha yah, aghāyur indriyārāmo mogham pārtha sa jīvati.'* (3.16)
- ***Meaning:*** 'He who does not follow the wheel of creation set in motion, indulging in the senses, lives a life of sin and waste, O Arjun.'
- **Connection:** This verse highlights the cyclical and interconnected nature of actions and outcomes. In project management, failing to understand and adapt to the cyclical and interdependent nature of processes leads to inefficiency and failure. Complexity in the PMBOK is often about managing such dynamic cycles effectively.

10. **Risk Management**

Let's talk about how the **Shrimad Bhagavad Gita** *connects to risk management in project management, particularly as described in the* **PMBOK**.

Take this verse:

'Yadricchaya chopapannam, swarga-dwaram apavritam' *(2.32)*
It means, 'Blessed are the warriors who face such challenges; they open the doors of heaven.'

Here, Krishna is encouraging Arjun to face challenges with courage and accept risks as part of his duty. In project management, risks are inevitable. But if we approach them with confidence and careful planning, we can turn obstacles into opportunities. That's exactly what Krishna is talking about—embracing challenges rather than avoiding them.

Other Verses and Their Connection to Risk Management

Another great verse is:

***'Karmanye vadhikaraste, aa phaleshu kadachana'** (2.47)*

It means, 'You have the right to perform your duty but not to the fruits of your actions.'

This is about focusing on what you can control. In risk management, you can't always control outcomes, but you can control how you identify and plan for risks. It's a reminder to act with diligence and let go of the anxiety about results.

Then there's:

***'Vimrishyaitad ashesena, yathecchasi tatha kuru'** (18.63),*

which translates to, 'Deliberate fully and then act as you wish.'

This verse highlights the importance of thinking things through—evaluating risks, understanding their impact and then making an informed decision. It's like Krishna's saying, 'Don't rush. Plan carefully and then act.'

How This Ties to Risk Management in PMBOK

Risk management is all about being proactive. Here's how we can approach it:

Identifying Risks

Use tools like brainstorming, SWOT analysis and root cause analysis to find risks early. Krishna's teachings about foresight fit perfectly here—be prepared for challenges even if they're not obvious yet.

Analysing Risks

Once you've identified risks, prioritise them with tools like the Probability and Impact Matrix. This is about focusing your energy on what matters most—just as Krishna advises Arjun to concentrate on his duty and not be distracted.

Creating Mitigation Plans

Short-Term Plans: *Deal with immediate risks, like backups or redundancies.*

Example: If a vendor is delayed, have an alternative vendor ready.

Benefit: *Quick solutions to keep the project moving.*

Long-Term Plans: *Aim to prevent future risks, like investing in training or improving processes.*

Example: Automating repetitive tasks to avoid errors.

Benefit: *Sustainable risk management and smoother operations.*

Handling Known-Unknown vs. Unknown-Unknown Risks

Known-Unknown Risks *are things you can predict but not fully control, like delivery delays.*

How to handle: Build contingency reserves or have backup plans.

Unknown-Unknown Risks *are surprises, like sudden regulatory changes.*

How to handle: Set aside management reserves and stay adaptable, like in Agile planning.

Krishna's advice about being prepared for uncertainties aligns well with these strategies—focus on what's within your control but be ready to handle surprises with grace.

Preventing Risks from Becoming Issues

One big part of risk management is stopping risks from turning into actual problems (or issues). To do that:

Monitor risks regularly. *Use tools like risk registers or dashboards to track them.*

Communicate early. *Make sure stakeholders and teams are aware of potential risks.*

Be proactive. *Look for early warning signs so you can act before it's too late.*

Krishna's emphasis on vigilance and readiness ties directly to this. He's basically saying: Keep your eyes open and be prepared to act.

Tools and Techniques

Some tools that really help in risk management are:

Risk Breakdown Structures (RBS): *Categorise risks to focus mitigation efforts.*

Decision Trees: *Evaluate different options and choose the best path.*

Earned Value Management (EVM): *Track cost and schedule variances to catch risks early.*

Why Risk Mitigation Matters

There are both ***short-term*** *and* ***long-term benefits*** *to having a solid mitigation plan:*

> ***Short-term:*** *You avoid disruptions and build confidence with stakeholders.*
>
> ***Long-term:*** *You improve project success rates and make your organisation more resilient.*

The ***Shrimad Bhagavad Gita*** *offers timeless advice for risk management. Krishna teaches us to embrace challenges, stay prepared and act decisively. By proactively addressing risks, planning mitigation strategies and staying vigilant, we can turn potential obstacles into opportunities for success—both in life and in projects.*

11. Adaptability and Resilience

Let's dive into the concept of **adaptability and resilience** and how the *Shrimad Bhagavad Gita* teaches us to handle challenges with a steady mind, which aligns beautifully with project management principles in PMBOK.

- ***Verse:*** *'Sukha-dukhe same kritva, labhalabhau jayajayau'* (2.38)
- ***Meaning:*** 'Treat happiness and distress, gain and loss, victory and defeat equally, and then engage in battle.'
- ***Connection:*** Krishna is advising Arjun to remain calm and composed, no matter the situation—be it success or failure, gain or loss. This mindset of equanimity is crucial for a project manager.

In project management, challenges like unexpected delays, cost overruns or shifting stakeholder priorities are inevitable. By staying adaptable and resilient, you can tackle these hurdles without losing focus on the bigger picture. Krishna's teaching reminds us that setbacks are part of the journey and not reasons to abandon the goal.

For instance, if a critical dependency fails, instead of panicking, a resilient project manager will adapt by re-prioritising tasks or finding alternative solutions. This adaptability ensures that the project remains on track, even in the face of adversity.

In PMBOK, adaptability and resilience are directly tied to **risk management**, **stakeholder management** and **change control.**

Risk Management:

Unexpected risks will always arise during a project. Krishna's teaching emphasises treating them as part of the process.

Tools like contingency planning and iterative risk reviews help build resilience to tackle such risks effectively.

Change Management:

Scope or stakeholder expectations may shift mid-project. Resilience means being flexible enough to pivot while maintaining focus on the project's core objectives.

Krishna's equanimity helps project managers remain calm when implementing change requests.

Stakeholder Management:

Managing diverse stakeholder needs can lead to conflicts or dissatisfaction. Adaptability allows a project manager to balance expectations and align everyone towards the project goals.

Other Verses That Teach Adaptability and Resilience

'Yoga-sthah kuru karmani, sangam tyaktva dhananjaya' **(2.48)**

Meaning: 'Be steadfast in the performance of your duty, O Arjun, abandoning attachment to success and failure. Such equanimity is called yoga.'

Relevance to PMBOK:

This verse emphasises staying focused on the process rather than being overly attached to the outcome. For a project manager, this translates to focusing on the project's **execution phase**, ensuring the team delivers quality work regardless of external pressures.

'Tasmad asaktah satatam karyam karma samachara' **(3.19)**

Meaning: 'Therefore, always perform your duty without attachment, for by doing so, one attains the Supreme.'

Relevance to PMBOK:

This verse highlights the importance of detachment from distractions. In project management, adaptability is about keeping the team aligned and focused on deliverables, even when external circumstances seem overwhelming.

***'Vidya-vinaya-sampanne, brahmane gavi hastini'* (5.18)**

Meaning: *'The wise see all beings as equal, be it a learned scholar, a cow, an elephant or a dog.'*

Relevance to PMBOK:

Adaptability also means managing diverse teams with fairness. As a project manager, treating all stakeholders and team members equally, regardless of their role, builds a collaborative and resilient work environment.

Practical Steps for Adaptability and Resilience in Projects

Be Proactive:

1. Anticipate risks using tools like SWOT analysis or risk registers.
2. Example: If a vendor is unreliable, identify alternatives early.

Stay Agile:

1. Use iterative frameworks like Agile or Scrum to adapt to changing requirements.
2. Example: Breaking deliverables into sprints allows for quick course correction if priorities change.

Encourage Open Communication:

1. Keep communication channels open for team members to report challenges.
2. Example: Conduct regular stand-ups or retrospectives to address issues.

Develop Mitigation Plans:

1. For known risks: Create contingency plans (e.g., allocate buffer time or resources).
2. For unknown risks: Keep a management reserve to handle surprises.

Focus on Long-Term Resilience:

1. Invest in team training and process improvements to reduce future risks.
2. Example: Upskill the team to handle new technologies or methodologies.

Build a Supportive Team Culture:

1. Foster a culture of collaboration and adaptability, ensuring the team feels supported in times of uncertainty.

Short- and Long-Term Benefits of Resilience

Short-Term:

- Quick recovery from setbacks.
- Smooth progress despite changes.

Long-Term:

- Improved stakeholder trust.
- Stronger project delivery capabilities.

The teachings of the ***Shrimad Bhagavad Gita*** on equanimity and detachment offer timeless wisdom for project managers. By staying calm, adaptable and resilient, you can navigate challenges and ensure project success. Remember, it's not about avoiding problems but facing them with the right mindset and tools—just like Krishna advises Arjun to embrace his duty, no matter the obstacles.

12. **Continuous Improvement**

- ***Verse:*** *'Uddhared atmanatmanam, na atmanam avasadayet' (6.5)*

  Meaning: *'Elevate yourself through the power of your mind and do not degrade yourself.'*

- ***Connection:*** *The essence of this verse emphasises personal growth and self-discipline, which aligns perfectly with the principle of continuous improvement. Krishna's teaching here is about taking charge of your progress through consistent effort, self-reflection and disciplined action. As project managers, this principle forms the foundation of how we approach our responsibilities.*

  Continuous improvement isn't a one-time activity—it's a mindset, a process that aligns beautifully with the PMBOK (Project Management Body of Knowledge) principles. Let me break it down for you:

  Alignment with PMBOK:

  PMBOK emphasises the **Plan-Do-Check-Act (PDCA)** *cycle, which is central to continuous improvement. This cycle ensures we plan effectively, execute, evaluate outcomes and make necessary adjustments.*

  In the **Monitor and Control** *process group, project managers actively track progress and identify areas for improvement.*

This aligns with Krishna's advice to elevate oneself through thoughtful, deliberate action.

The ***Lessons Learned Repository****—a key tool in the PMBOK—is an excellent example of how continuous reflection and improvement can lead to better outcomes in future projects.*

Other Shrimad Bhagavad Gita Verses on Continuous Improvement:

Verse 2.50: *'Yogah karmasu kaushalam'*

Meaning: 'Yoga is skill in action.'

Yoga *refers to a state of union, balance or mindfulness. It's not limited to physical postures but is about aligning the mind, body and soul towards a higher purpose. In my honest opinion, 'Yoga' is the ability to prioritise our goals above all else and stay focused until you achieve it. Of course, to achieve goals, our mind, body and soul must be aligned…*

Karmasu *means 'in actions' or ' performing one's duties.'*

Kaushalam *translates to 'excellence,' 'skillfulness' or 'efficiency.'*

Explanation: *In project management, skillful execution of tasks—through refined techniques, effective tools and ethical practices—is crucial. This verse reinforces the need for learning new methods and applying them with precision.*

Verse 18.48: *'Saha-jam karma kaunteya sa-dosham api na tyajet'*

Meaning: *'One should not abandon work, even if it is imperfect.'*

Explanation: *No project is flawless, but the key is to identify imperfections, improve processes and aim for better results in subsequent efforts.*

Practical Steps for Continuous Improvement:

- ***Pursue Relevant Courses and Certifications:***

  To enhance your skills and stay current, invest in certifications like:

- ***Technical Certifications:***
  - *PMP (Project Management Professional)*
  - *CSM (Certified ScrumMaster)*
  - *ITIL (Information Technology Infrastructure Library)*

- ***Management Certifications:***
  - *Lean Six Sigma (Green/Black Belt)*
  - *Business Analysis (CBAP or PMI-PBA)*
  - *SAFe Agile Certification*

  These certifications not only build your technical expertise but also improve your ability to lead teams and deliver value.

- ***Stay Updated with Market Trends:***

  Be proactive in understanding industry shifts, emerging technologies and best practices by:

  Subscribing to newsletters like Gartner, McKinsey or PMI.

  Participating in webinars and conferences.

  Following thought leaders in your domain.

- ***Understand Your Customer and Industry:***

  Knowing your customer's sector is key to delivering tailored solutions. Research their market, competitors and regulatory environment. Engage with stakeholders regularly to align project goals with their strategic objectives.

- ***Foster a Culture of Feedback and Learning:***

  Conduct ***retrospectives*** *after each project phase to capture lessons learned.*

  Use tools like root cause analysis to address recurring issues.

  Empower your team with training programmes to enhance their capabilities.

- ***Leverage Technology:***

  Invest in project management tools like Jira, Asana or MS Project to streamline workflows.

  Use analytics tools to measure performance and identify improvement areas.

- ***Practice Self-Reflection and Growth:***

  Incorporate mindfulness practices such as journalling or meditation.

  Regularly evaluate your performance and set actionable goals for improvement.

  Krishna's teachings emphasise that growth is a continuous journey, and it begins with disciplined effort and a clear focus. By aligning these principles with PMBOK, pursuing certifications and staying current with market trends, project managers can truly elevate their skills, deliver quality and add meaningful value. The Shrimad Bhagavad Gita reminds us that excellence is not a destination but a constant pursuit.

Throughout this chapter, we have explored the twelve principles of project management as outlined in the PMBOK, understanding each in isolation and examining its relevance in guiding projects towards successful outcomes. To conclude, it is illuminating to see how all these principles can operate together in a single cohesive narrative, drawn from the early life of Lord Krishna. His childhood in Gokul and Vrindavan, though often recounted as playful adventures and miraculous feats, offers profound lessons on leadership, strategy and project management that are surprisingly applicable even to modern enterprise-level projects.

Even as a child, Krishna displayed an innate understanding of value. He recognised what was most important to his community—the safety of the villagers, the well-being of the cows and the overall harmony of the village. Every action he undertook, whether defending the inhabitants from threats or ensuring resources were protected, reflected a deep commitment to safeguarding and enhancing value. This early awareness mirrors the modern project management principle of managing value, ensuring that every decision contributes meaningfully to the ultimate objectives of a project.

Krishna also exemplified the art of stakeholder engagement. From Yashoda and Nanda Maharaj to the villagers and fellow cowherds, he consistently listened to concerns, understood fears and communicated plans with clarity. In times of uncertainty—when demons threatened or when Kamsa's interference loomed—Krishna kept stakeholders informed and aligned, fostering trust and collaboration. This early practice mirrors the modern project manager's need to maintain engagement and alignment with stakeholders, ensuring that everyone understands both challenges and objectives.

From his earliest exploits, Krishna demonstrated the importance of enabling team performance. He along with his elder brother, Lord Balrama, collaborated with friends and allies, such as villagers and other cowherd children from the same and nearby villages, assigning tasks according to each person's strengths. Whether coordinating efforts to protect the cows from thieves or devising strategies to overcome demonic threats, Krishna empowered his team to take ownership of their roles while guiding them towards a common goal. This nurturing of talent and delegation of responsibility reflects the PMBOK principle of optimising team performance to achieve desired outcomes.

Leadership, in Krishna's life, was never about personal glory but about inspiration and guidance. Whether lifting the Govardhan Hill to shield villagers from torrential rains or subduing Kaliya the serpent to cleanse the Yamuna, Krishna's courage and vision motivated others to act, instilling confidence and clarity even in moments of crisis. His leadership was adaptable, demonstrating the necessity to tailor approaches to suit the situation. No two challenges were met with the same strategy; each required careful consideration of context, resources and constraints, highlighting the need to customise methods for optimal results.

Krishna's commitment to quality and excellence was evident in every undertaking. While safeguarding his community or managing resources, he ensured that all efforts were efficient, effective and sustainable. At the same time, he continuously analysed the complexity of situations, anticipating potential challenges and preparing appropriate responses. From assessing demon behaviour to planning village-wide protective measures, Krishna managed complexity with foresight, an approach directly relevant to navigating intricate modern projects.

Equally remarkable was Krishna's mastery of uncertainty and risk. Life in Gokul was unpredictable, with sudden threats from natural elements, demons or human adversaries. Krishna approached each situation with calculated foresight, preparing contingencies, evaluating possible outcomes and acting decisively. In doing so, he demonstrated the principle of risk-based decision-making, while also optimising time, effort and resources—a clear reflection of the triple constraint concept, even in the midst of chaos.

Throughout these experiences, Krishna continuously integrated learning into his actions. He observed, reflected and applied lessons from each encounter to improve subsequent strategies. This ability to capture insights, adapt tactics and refine approaches mirrors knowledge management practices in enterprise projects today. Moreover, Krishna's actions were always outcome-focused. Whether ensuring the safety of his community, the protection of livestock or the restoration of harmony, he maintained a clear vision of what success looked like, demonstrating the importance of outcome-oriented project management.

Finally, Krishna's ethical and professional conduct underpinned every endeavour. Even when confronting danger or chaos, he acted with integrity, fairness and righteousness. This steadfast commitment to ethical principles ensured that his strategies were not only effective but aligned with higher moral and societal standards, reinforcing the timeless PMBOK principle of professional responsibility.

Viewed holistically, Krishna's childhood provides a living illustration of how all twelve PMBOK principles can function together in practice. Leadership, stakeholder engagement, tailoring approaches, risk management, quality, value delivery and ethics are not separate actions but interconnected aspects of effective management. Just as Krishna balanced multiple threats, stakeholders and constraints to achieve harmony and safety in Gokul and Vrindavan, modern project managers must integrate these principles to navigate complex, enterprise-level projects successfully.

In essence, Krishna's life, even in its playful and miraculous moments, demonstrates that project management principles are universal, timeless and actionable at every level of endeavor. By internalising these lessons, project managers and leaders can transform challenges into opportunities, align teams with purpose and deliver extraordinary results—whether on the battlefield, in the corporate world or in the broader journey of life itself.

8 Performance Domains

The addition of performance domains to the PMBOK Guide (Seventh Edition) reflects the evolving nature of project management, moving beyond rigid processes to embrace a more holistic, value-driven approach. In the past, project management often emphasised following prescribed steps, which sometimes limited flexibility. Performance domains address this by shifting the focus to achieving desired outcomes, allowing project managers to tailor practices to their specific contexts. They also align with the modern emphasis on delivering value, recognising that project success is no longer just about completing tasks on time and within budget—it's about meeting stakeholder expectations and aligning with organisational goals. By encouraging adaptability, the domains provide a structure that works across diverse methodologies, whether Agile, hybrid or traditional. Furthermore, they simplify project management by moving away from overly complex processes and focusing instead on key performance areas, making it easier to manage projects effectively. Importantly, these domains reflect current trends in the field, such as stakeholder engagement, team collaboration and sustainability, which are essential in today's dynamic environments. In essence, performance domains represent a shift towards outcome-oriented, flexible and comprehensive project management practices, equipping managers to navigate the complexities of modern projects while consistently delivering value.

1. **Stakeholder Performance**

    - ***Verse:*** *'Yo mam pasyati sarvatra, Sarvam cha mayi pasyati'* (6.30)
    - ***Meaning:*** 'One who sees me in everything and everything in me is never lost to me.'

- ***Connection:*** This verse from the *Shrimad Bhagavad Gita* speaks to the profound principle of interconnectedness—the idea that everything in the universe is linked and that each element must be understood as part of a greater whole. Krishna's teachings underscore that by recognising the interconnectedness of all things, one achieves a deeper understanding and can effectively navigate life's complexities. Similarly, in the context of project management, stakeholder engagement is not a standalone activity but a continuous, interconnected process that influences every facet of the project. A successful project manager must learn to perceive the needs, expectations and concerns of stakeholders from a broader, more inclusive perspective, ensuring that the project serves the diverse interests of all parties while remaining aligned with the organisation's overarching goals.

Stakeholders in a project can range from clients and sponsors to team members, regulators, suppliers and end users. Each stakeholder has their own set of needs, expectations and interests, which can often be diverse or even conflicting. If a project manager fails to recognise and address these varying expectations, there's a high risk that the project's plans, strategies and frameworks will become misaligned with actual stakeholder needs. This misalignment can lead to dissatisfaction, resistance and even the potential failure of the project. Krishna's verse serves as a powerful reminder that everything is part of a larger system. In stakeholder management, it's essential to see the bigger picture, ensuring that no stakeholder is overlooked and that the project stays on track.

Key Takeaways from Krishna's Teachings on Stakeholder Engagement:

- **The Importance of Holistic Stakeholder Engagement**

Krishna's guidance stresses the need to see everything in its interrelated form, and this wisdom can be applied directly to how project managers engage with stakeholders. Stakeholder management should not be viewed as a separate task or a one-off activity but as an ongoing, dynamic process that impacts every stage of the project. It requires consistent effort and proactive engagement—understanding stakeholders' expectations, aligning them with project goals and adjusting strategies based on feedback.

Failure to acknowledge and address stakeholder concerns at any stage—be it during planning, execution or decision-making—can lead to severe consequences. This oversight can result in derailed projects, missed deadlines, cost overruns or compromised quality. These are classic failures in the triple constraints of scope, time and cost, which often arise from neglecting the true needs and expectations of stakeholders. The result is a dissatisfied customer or stakeholder, which undermines the success of the project, even if it is technically completed.

- **Proactive Stakeholder Management**

Krishna's verse emphasises the interconnectedness of everything, urging us to view all parts of a system through a unified lens. In stakeholder management, this means actively seeking out feedback and continuously engaging with stakeholders throughout the project lifecycle. A project manager's role is not only to lead the project but to ensure that all stakeholders are regularly consulted, that their concerns are heard and that their feedback is integrated into the project plan. This kind of engagement prevents misunderstandings and ensures that the project evolves in alignment with stakeholder expectations.

Proactive stakeholder management can mitigate the risks of resistance, misunderstandings and misalignment. It involves regular communication, transparent updates and, most importantly, fostering a sense of ownership and involvement among stakeholders, which enhances collaboration and drives commitment to the project's success.

- **Alignment of Stakeholder Interests with Project Goals**

One of the most significant challenges in project management is ensuring that stakeholder interests align with the project's broader goals. If stakeholders feel that their needs are not being considered or that their expectations are not being met, resistance will inevitably arise. Krishna's teachings offer a powerful lesson here. Just as he guided Arjun to align his emotions and concerns with the larger purpose of the war, a project manager must help stakeholders align their interests with the project's ultimate vision. This alignment helps prevent conflicts, reduces resistance and encourages the active support of all parties involved.

For instance, if a stakeholder feels disconnected from the project or its goals, they may become disengaged or obstructive. A project manager's task is to bridge these gaps, ensuring that stakeholders understand how the project's outcomes benefit them and that their needs are met within the scope of the project.

- **Example from the Mahabharata: Krishna's Stakeholder Management**

Krishna's own actions in the Mahabharata provide a powerful example of exceptional stakeholder management. One of the most notable instances is his approach to Arjun's dilemma before the great Kurukshetra battle. Arjun, a key stakeholder in the conflict, was deeply conflicted about fighting his own family members. Krishna did not dismiss Arjun's emotions or force him into action. Instead, he engaged with Arjun's concerns with deep empathy and strategic foresight, aligning Arjun's duties with the larger vision of restoring righteousness. By guiding Arjun through his internal conflict and helping him reconnect with his sense of duty (*dharma*), Krishna enabled Arjun to overcome his hesitation and re-engage in the battle, leading to the ultimate success of the Pandavas.

In project management, this example highlights the importance of empathetic engagement and alignment. A project manager who listens to stakeholder concerns, addresses them with respect and aligns their needs with the broader project goals will foster greater cooperation and commitment, ensuring project success.

- **Conclusion**

By embracing Krishna's holistic vision of interconnectedness, project managers can cultivate stronger, more effective stakeholder engagement. Seeing everything as part of a larger system allows managers to address stakeholder concerns comprehensively and ensure that the project stays aligned with its overarching goals. Just as Krishna ensured Arjun's commitment to his duty by helping him see the bigger picture, project managers must align their stakeholders' concerns with the project's vision to gain their commitment and drive the project to success. Through proactive engagement, alignment of interests and a holistic approach to stakeholder management, projects can be delivered successfully, meeting the needs of all involved parties.

2. **Team Performance**

    - ***Verse:*** *'Tasmaat sarveshu kaleshu, mam anusmara yudhya cha'* (8.7)
    - ***Meaning:*** 'Therefore, always think of me and perform your duty.'

    This verse reinforces that great teamwork is built on vision, dedication and purposeful action—qualities that define successful project execution.

    - ***Connection:*** This verse from the *Shrimad Bhagavad Gita* offers profound guidance on team performance, emphasising that great teamwork is rooted in vision, dedication and purposeful action—qualities essential for successful project execution. Krishna's advice to Arjun to keep the higher purpose in mind while performing his duties can be directly applied to managing high-performing teams in any project.

      Krishna's teachings reinforce the importance of aligning one's actions with a greater vision. Similarly, in project management, the role of the leader is not just to direct tasks but to ensure that the entire team is aligned with the project's broader objectives and goals. Just as Arjun was reminded to stay focused on his duty, project managers must keep their teams motivated and clear about the purpose of their work.

A high-performing team is not simply a collection of individuals working in isolation—it is a **collective unit**, all working in harmony towards a shared goal, with clarity and commitment.

By consistently reinforcing the project's vision and objectives, leaders can cultivate a sense of **purpose**, **dedication** and **accountability** within the team. This sense of shared purpose is what propels teams towards successful outcomes, ensuring that each member's contribution is valued and aligned with the larger mission.

Key Takeaways from Krishna's Guidance for Team Performance:

- **Clarity of Purpose**

Just as Krishna urges Arjun to act with full awareness of his duty, project managers must ensure that every team member understands their role, responsibilities and how their contributions align with the overall goals of the project. This sense of clarity ensures that everyone is moving in the same direction, with a shared understanding of the project's purpose and long-term objectives.

A well-defined purpose acts as a compass, guiding teams through the complexities of the project lifecycle. When team members see the bigger picture and understand how their work contributes to the final outcome, they are more likely to remain engaged, motivated and focused on achieving project success.

- **Consistency and Focus**

One of the critical components of successful team performance is consistency. Krishna's teachings encourage Arjun to remain focused on his duty, regardless of external challenges. Similarly, project managers must foster a culture of **focus** within the team, ensuring that everyone is aligned with the project's priorities and objectives. This focus prevents distractions and inefficiencies, streamlining workflows and improving productivity.

Encouraging consistent effort towards the end goal is crucial, especially when projects face shifts in scope, resources or timelines. A focused team is better equipped to handle unexpected changes and deliver results on time, without losing momentum.

- **Resilience in Challenges**

Krishna's message to Arjun about persevering in the face of difficulties is highly relevant to project teams navigating uncertainties and obstacles. Project managers must instil resilience within their teams, encouraging them to anchor decisions in the project's purpose and remain committed, even when faced with challenges.

Just as Arjun was encouraged to stay committed to his duty, project teams should be prepared to stay the course, despite setbacks. Whether it's scope changes, resource limitations or unforeseen risks, a resilient team remains adaptable and focused on finding solutions rather than being overwhelmed by challenges.

- **Motivation and Engagement**

Krishna's teaching to Arjun is a reminder of the importance of **engagement** and **motivation**. By regularly reminding their team of the significance of their work and the broader purpose it serves, leaders can foster a deep sense of responsibility and pride within the team. This emotional connection to the project's objectives boosts engagement and encourages collaboration among team members.

A motivated team performs better because each individual is not just completing a task—they are actively contributing to a larger mission. This sense of responsibility translates into higher productivity, better teamwork and improved outcomes across the board.

- **Conclusion**

By following the wisdom found in Krishna's guidance to Arjun, project managers can cultivate a **high-performing team** that is focused, resilient and deeply connected to the project's goals. Through **clarity of purpose**, **consistent focus**, **resilience in the face of challenges** and a strong sense of **motivation and engagement**, teams can overcome obstacles and achieve the successful execution of the project. Just as Krishna's teachings helped Arjun stay committed to his duties, effective project leadership helps teams stay aligned with the greater vision, ensuring their success.

3. **Development Approach and Life Cycle**

    - ***Verse:*** *'Asanshaya mahabaho, mano durnigraham chalam'* (6.35)

    - ***Meaning***: 'The mind is restless and difficult to control, but it can be subdued by practice and detachment.'

    - ***Connection:*** This verse, with its profound wisdom, offers significant insights into the **development approach** and **life cycle** of a project, particularly in environments characterised by complexity and change. Just as the mind is prone to distraction and requires discipline to maintain focus, the process of project development demands structured yet adaptable methodologies to address the evolving nature of requirements, uncertainties and unforeseen risks.

Key Insights in Project Development from This Verse:

- **Flexibility in Choosing the Right Approach**

Krishna emphasises the importance of practice and detachment, which can be directly applied to selecting and refining project development methodologies. A **rigid mindset** can severely limit progress, whereas a **flexible approach** allows teams to iterate, improve and adapt in response to challenges and evolving demands.

For example:

1. **Agile methodologies** are centred around iterative development, allowing teams to adjust based on feedback and evolving business needs. This fosters continuous improvement, learning and responsiveness to change.
2. **Waterfall models**, in contrast, are highly effective for projects with **well-defined requirements**, where consistency, stability and structure take precedence. They provide a clear, linear path when project scope is unlikely to change.
3. **Hybrid approaches** combine elements of both Agile and Waterfall, ensuring that there is enough structure for predictability while also offering flexibility to adapt as new information or challenges arise.

Just as Krishna teaches the importance of practice to control the mind, project managers must practice adaptability in choosing the most appropriate development approach, ensuring it is in alignment with the project's needs, scope and external factors.

- **Mindfulness in Managing Complexity**

In the same way that Krishna advises discipline over the wandering mind, managing complexity in project development requires a **mindful approach**. Teams must focus on **structured processes**, **regular retrospectives** and **clear priorities** to stay aligned with the project's goals. Managing complexity effectively involves balancing several factors simultaneously, such as **scope**, **time**, **cost** and **quality**.

Mindfulness in decision-making helps project teams avoid knee-jerk reactions and the temptation to rush through challenges. Instead, teams are better equipped to stay grounded, think strategically and make informed decisions that move the project forward without becoming overwhelmed by its complexities. Just as Krishna teaches how controlling the mind brings clarity and focus, applying mindfulness ensures a more balanced, effective approach to managing project development.

- **The Power of Continuous Improvement**

Krishna's advice to refine the mind through discipline and detachment mirrors the principle of **continuous improvement** in project development. In methodologies such as **Agile**, teams regularly reflect on their work, assess progress and adapt their processes to enhance efficiency. This cycle of improvement enables the team to grow and refine their approach, just as Krishna encourages consistent mental discipline to achieve mastery.

In the development cycle, tools like **Scrum** and **Kanban** emphasise regular retrospectives, sprint reviews and refinement. These practices allow teams to review their progress in short intervals, identify bottlenecks or areas of improvement and adapt accordingly. By fostering a culture of continuous learning and improvement, teams can enhance their overall performance and create more successful outcomes.

- **Detachment from Fixed Outcomes**

Krishna's teachings on **detachment from outcomes** apply directly to the unpredictable nature of project development. In projects, especially those involving innovation or complex requirements, sticking rigidly to a predetermined plan can often be counterproductive. As Krishna advises, the path to success lies in not clinging too tightly to the outcome but rather focusing on the **incremental progress** made along the way.

Teams that embrace detachment from fixed outcomes are more open to **evolving requirements** and changing conditions. This mindset allows project managers and teams to remain agile, adjust priorities as needed, and be more resilient to disruptions or shifting expectations. By focusing on continual progress and being willing to adapt, teams ensure that the project moves forward, regardless of the challenges or changes that arise.

- **Practical Application in Project Development**

Agile Teams: Agile teams conduct **sprint reviews** and **retrospectives** to refine their approach, reflect on what went well and adapt their strategies accordingly. This continuous feedback loop helps the team stay aligned with the evolving needs of the project.

Minimum Viable Product (MVP): Product development teams follow **MVP strategies**, releasing products early to gather feedback, learn and iterate. This approach allows teams to build, test and adjust in real-time, based on user feedback.

Risk Management: Instead of adhering strictly to outdated plans, teams practice **proactive adjustments** in response to risks and uncertainties. This flexible mindset ensures that the team is prepared to pivot or refine its strategy as circumstances change.

- **Conclusion**

By integrating the wisdom of **discipline**, **adaptability** and **reflection**, project teams can navigate the complexities of development with greater clarity and focus. Just as Krishna assures Arjun that the restless mind can be controlled through conscious effort and practice, project teams too can master the challenges of development by maintaining the right balance of structure and flexibility. With this approach, they can overcome the uncertainties inherent in any project while staying aligned with their ultimate goal: delivering successful and impactful outcomes.

4. **Planning Performance**

   - ***Verse:*** *'Jnanam te ham sa-vijnanam, idam vakshyamy asesatah'* (7.2)
   - ***Meaning:*** 'I shall now explain to you both knowledge and wisdom.'
   - ***Connection:*** This verse encapsulates the essence of combining both **theoretical knowledge** (*jnanam*) and **practical wisdom** (*vijnanam*). These principles are not just spiritual teachings but also directly applicable to **project planning** in management. The success of any project does not solely depend on facts, data or structured processes—it also requires the practical application of experience, foresight and insightful judgement. This blending of knowledge and wisdom

is what allows projects to be planned effectively and executed successfully.

Key Insights in Project Planning from This Verse:

- **Balancing Knowledge (Data) and Wisdom (Experience)**

Jnanam **(Knowledge)** in project planning refers to structured data, established best practices, industry standards and methodologies such as the **PMBOK**, **Agile frameworks** and **Lean principles**. These are the tools and facts that guide the planning process, providing a clear structure for scope, budget and timelines.

Vijnanam **(Wisdom)**, on the other hand, is gained through hands-on experience. It comes from lessons learned in past projects, understanding team dynamics and having the ability to anticipate challenges and risks that cannot always be predicted by data alone. This wisdom also involves recognising when deviations from the plan might be necessary and adapting the approach accordingly.

A successful project plan must integrate both. While data-driven decisions provide structure and clarity, the experience gained through previous projects helps anticipate unforeseen risks and constraints, allowing the plan to be robust yet adaptable.

- **The Art of Strategic Thinking**

Krishna doesn't simply provide knowledge—he ensures that Arjun understands how to apply it in the context of battle. Similarly, in project management, planning is not merely about establishing timelines, budgets and scope; it is about **strategically aligning resources**, anticipating dependencies and preparing for potential obstacles.

Strategic thinking in planning goes beyond ticking off boxes. It involves understanding the **big picture** and ensuring that resources are used in the most efficient and effective way. Just like Krishna's teachings help Arjun apply wisdom on the battlefield, strategic planning guides project managers to make decisions that align with long-term objectives, even when faced with uncertainty or change.

- **Holistic and Adaptive Planning**

A **rigid, knowledge-only approach** to planning can lead to failure, especially in the face of uncertainties. On the other hand, a **wisdom-driven, flexible mindset** allows the plan to evolve as real-world changes unfold.

For example, in software development, traditional **waterfall methods** emphasise detailed upfront planning based on data (knowledge-based). However, **Agile methodologies** focus more on iterative learning, which incorporates real-time feedback and adjustments based on practical experiences (wisdom-based). This flexibility allows teams to adapt their approach as the project progresses, without losing sight of the end goal.

In reality, a **hybrid approach** often works best. By blending structured planning with the flexibility to adapt, project managers can navigate both predictable and unpredictable challenges, ensuring the project stays on course.

- **Risk Management and Contingency Planning**

Krishna imparts wisdom to Arjun to prepare him for the inevitable battle challenges. Similarly, effective project planning requires a thorough understanding of potential risks and the development of contingency plans to mitigate these risks.

Good planning doesn't just set goals—it prepares for **what could go wrong**. By identifying **potential risks** upfront, assessing their impact and implementing **mitigation strategies**, project managers can reduce the likelihood of disruptions.

For example, project teams often use **risk registers** to track potential issues, while **scenario analysis** helps prepare for different possible outcomes. Keeping **buffer resources** for unexpected delays and changes further strengthens the project's resilience.

- **Clear Communication and Stakeholder Alignment**

Just as Krishna takes time to explain profound truths to Arjun, **project managers must communicate their plans** clearly and consistently to stakeholders. Clear communication ensures that everyone involved in the project understands the plan, their role in its execution and the objectives to be achieved. This alignment fosters:

Transparency—stakeholders know what to expect and when.

Collaboration—everyone works together towards common goals.

Trust in execution—when the plan is communicated clearly, it enhances confidence in the project's success.

Effective communication is an essential part of both planning and execution. It ensures that all stakeholders are aligned and informed, which helps mitigate misunderstandings and promotes smoother project delivery.

- **Practical Application of This Wisdom in Planning**

Blend Data and Experience: Use analytics and structured data-driven tools, but also tap into the team's collective experience to inform decisions.

Think Strategically: Go beyond short-term goals. Ensure the plan aligns with both immediate deliverables and long-term impact, considering future implications.

Stay Flexible: Be open to adapting the plan as new information becomes available. The world is constantly changing, and the plan must remain adaptable to meet evolving demands.

Prepare for Risks: Identify and assess potential disruptions early on and have mitigation strategies in place. The more prepared you are for the unexpected, the less likely it is to derail the project.

Communicate Clearly: Ensure all stakeholders understand the plan, their roles and the overall objectives. This fosters trust, collaboration and transparency.

- **Conclusion**

By combining both **knowledge (data-driven planning)** and **wisdom (experience-based decision-making)**, project managers can develop plans that are not only well-informed but also flexible and adaptable. Just as Krishna taught Arjun the delicate balance between theory and practice, the same principle applies to project management. A great project manager ensures that their plans are not only grounded in solid data but are also shaped by experience, intuition and strategic thinking. This combination of knowledge and wisdom leads to successful project execution and long-term project success.

5. **Project Work Performance**

- ***Verse:*** *'Yogah karmasu kaushalam'* (2.50)
- ***Meaning:*** 'Yoga is skill in action.'

- ***Connection:*** In Krishna's teachings, 'skill in action' is referred to as yoga. This principle of skill and mindfulness in action can be applied directly to various performance domains within project management, particularly **Managing Project Work**, **Team Performance** and the process of transitioning the project to Business As Usual (BAU). Krishna's message emphasises the importance of performing tasks with competence, focus and awareness, which extends beyond the completion of the project itself and into the critical phase of transferring ownership and responsibility for project deliverables.

- **Managing Project Work**

Managing project work is not just about overseeing daily tasks but also ensuring that the project reaches a successful conclusion. This involves a structured and effective **handover** of the project to the operational teams, where the results, deliverables and knowledge generated are seamlessly integrated into the regular business operations. Krishna's emphasis on skill and expertise in action is especially relevant here, as it encourages project managers and teams to be mindful of the importance of closure.

Effective project closure involves transferring not just the tangible deliverables but also the tools, lessons learned and knowledge created during the project. By applying Krishna's teachings, project managers are guided to ensure that the project's final products are in good shape and that their value continues in the operational phase. This smooth transition requires careful documentation and a clear communication process, where the new custodians of the project outcomes are well-equipped to maintain and further develop them.

- **Team Performance**

A successful transition to BAU hinges on the performance of the project team. A team that performs with competence, focus and mindfulness—as Krishna advocates—ensures that the work is not just completed but is documented and shared in a way that allows others to take over seamlessly. **High-performing teams** play a crucial role in ensuring that their knowledge, strategies and decisions are effectively communicated so that those taking over the project can pick up where they left off.

This principle of 'yoga' in action means that teams must work not only to deliver the project's outputs but also to prepare for the sustainability of those outputs after the project ends. The act of transferring knowledge effectively, whether through documentation or knowledge-sharing sessions, becomes a key responsibility of the team. In doing so, they help ensure that the project's results are not just handed off but continue to function smoothly and evolve over time.

- **Quality Management**

In the transition from the project to BAU, **quality management** plays a crucial role in ensuring that the project deliverables meet the required standards. Krishna's teachings on 'quality in action' suggest that the work should not only be completed but must also be of the highest possible standard, ready for operational use without disruption. This aligns with the need for all project deliverables to be stable, functional and thoroughly documented.

As part of the transition process, project managers must ensure that the final outputs are of exceptional quality and are easily transferable to the operations team. This includes checking that the deliverables meet the quality criteria set at the start of the project and that any gaps or improvements are addressed. Effective quality management ensures that the project's outputs can be maintained, scaled and improved upon in the future, minimising disruptions in day-to-day operations.

- **Conclusion**

Krishna's principle of skillful action—performing duties with competence, focus and dedication—extends throughout the lifecycle of a project, from its execution to its closure and transition into business operations. By focusing on managing project work, ensuring high-performing teams and maintaining high-quality standards, project managers can ensure a smooth handover of the project to BAU. This approach not only ensures that the project delivers its intended outcomes but also that these outcomes continue to create value for the organisation in the long term.

6. **Delivery Performance**

   - ***Verse:*** *'Tyaktva karma-phala-sangam, nityatrupto nirashrayah'* (4.20)
   - ***Meaning:*** 'By renouncing attachment to the fruits of action, one attains supreme peace.'
   - ***Connection:*** Krishna's teachings about renouncing attachment to the outcomes of actions offer profound insights into the **Delivery Performance** domain in project management. The focus in this domain is on executing project work effectively and efficiently, with an emphasis on the quality of effort rather than becoming overly attached to or distracted by the results. Krishna's wisdom encourages project teams

and managers to prioritise the process itself and work with dedication, irrespective of the final outcome.

- **Focus on the Process (Execution over Outcome)**

In project management, **Delivery Performance** is all about ensuring the efficient execution of the project, whether it is about managing the scope, adhering to timelines or allocating resources effectively. Krishna's teachings on detachment urge project managers and teams to focus on executing their tasks with commitment, skill and diligence, rather than becoming fixated on the final outcome.

When project teams shift their attention to the process—ensuring quality, managing risks and meeting deadlines—rather than constantly worrying about uncertainties or the final result, it leads to a more relaxed and productive work environment. This approach helps mitigate stress, avoid burnout and sustain energy throughout the delivery phase. It encourages teams to trust the process, knowing that consistent effort will eventually lead to the desired outcome, even if the journey has its ups and downs.

- **Resilience and Clarity**

One of the core elements of Krishna's message is the cultivation of mental clarity and resilience. In the project delivery phase, where obstacles like scope changes, unforeseen risks and tight deadlines are common, this philosophy becomes particularly useful. The ability to stay grounded and committed to the task at hand—without becoming emotionally overwhelmed by the fluctuations in outcomes—enhances the team's ability to deliver successfully.

Resilience is key here; as projects often involve shifting circumstances, maintaining composure in the face of adversity allows project managers to steer the team through difficulties with confidence. Krishna's teachings encourage us to remain calm and focused, trusting that steady, well-executed actions will lead to the desired results. For project managers, this means supporting the team to stay focused on the work rather than getting discouraged or distracted by challenges.

- **Sustaining Motivation and Commitment**

Krishna's teachings also provide a blueprint for maintaining motivation during the course of the project. When project teams focus on delivering quality work and not on the potential rewards or the outcome itself, they are more likely to remain engaged and motivated. Detaching from the outcome frees the team from the pressure of constant performance evaluation, allowing them to concentrate on the task at hand.

This mindset fosters a healthier team dynamic, as it encourages collaboration, innovation and problem-solving. It also reduces the fear of failure, helping to create an environment where team members are more willing to take initiative and work together towards successful project delivery. When the team remains committed to the process and its intrinsic value, it leads to higher-quality work and greater satisfaction with the overall project.

- **Continuous Improvement**

Another powerful insight from Krishna's philosophy is the concept of continuous improvement, which is crucial in **Delivery Performance**. By focusing on improving actions without becoming overly concerned with external validation or the outcome, project teams are empowered to innovate and refine their processes. Krishna's teachings encourage a mindset where every action, no matter how small, becomes an opportunity for growth and development.

When teams detach from the fear of failure or success, they open themselves up to experimentation and learning, fostering a culture of innovation and ongoing refinement. This leads to long-term success, as teams continuously adapt to new challenges and improve their delivery performance. For project managers, this means encouraging reflection after each project phase and applying lessons learned to future work.

- **Conclusion**

Applying Krishna's philosophy of renouncing attachment to the results can lead to enhanced clarity, focus and resilience during the delivery phase. When project teams embrace this mindset, they are more likely to stay committed to high performance, regardless of external outcomes or uncertainties. The process becomes the priority, and with steady, quality execution, the final outcome will take care of itself. This approach ultimately fosters a more sustainable and effective delivery process, driving the team towards success while maintaining their well-being and commitment to the project.

7. **Measurement Performance**

    - ***Verse:*** *'Vidya-vinaya-sampanne, brahmane gavi hastini'* (5.18)

    - ***Meaning:*** 'The humble sages see with equal vision a learned Brahmana, a cow, an elephant, a dog and a dog-eater.'

- ***Connection:*** Krishna's teaching of seeing all beings with equal vision offers profound guidance for the **Measurement Performance** domain in project management. Just as the sage in this verse treats all beings impartially, project performance must be assessed without bias, based solely on objective, predefined criteria. This ensures fairness, consistency and transparency—key elements necessary for accurate assessments and sound decision-making throughout the project lifecycle.

- **Impartiality in Measurement**

Krishna's message of impartiality encourages us to view all beings equally, regardless of their social status, role or background. In the realm of project management, this principle translates into evaluating performance based on measurable, factual data, rather than subjective opinions or favoritism. Whether the task is small or large, whether it is handled by a senior team member or a junior, the evaluation should be consistent.

By measuring project performance using predefined metrics such as time, cost, quality and scope, project managers ensure that all aspects of the project are held to the same standard. This approach eliminates biases that might arise from personal perceptions or external pressures, providing an objective basis for judgement. It ensures that decisions made throughout the project are fair and aligned with the project's overall goals.

- **Objective Criteria Over Subjective Judgements**

Krishna teaches us to focus on impartiality, which directly relates to assessing project performance based on quantifiable and predefined criteria. Project performance should not be evaluated based on feelings or personal preferences but rather on measurable factors that are agreed upon in advance. Tools like **Key Performance Indicators (KPIs)**, **Earned Value Management (EVM)** and **performance reviews** are all grounded in objective data, offering a factual approach to performance evaluation.

By relying on such tools, project managers minimise the risk of misjudgement or personal biases affecting their decisions. Instead, they make data-driven choices that are fair, transparent and in alignment with the objectives of the project. This ensures that all stakeholders—whether team members, clients or sponsors—are evaluated on the same basis, contributing to the project's credibility and success.

- **Fairness and Transparency**

One of Krishna's key lessons is the importance of fairness and transparency, both of which are vital in the measurement of project performance. When performance is measured impartially, it fosters trust among the team and stakeholders alike. Every individual, regardless of their role or seniority, should be evaluated according to the same standards. This impartial approach not only supports transparency but also creates an open, collaborative environment where feedback is based on facts, not favoritism or assumptions.

Transparent measurement processes encourage accountability, ensuring that all team members are aware of their performance and any areas where improvement is necessary. It also ensures that the project's progress is clear to external stakeholders, building trust and confidence throughout the project lifecycle.

- **Consistency in Evaluation**

Krishna's teaching of equal vision extends to the consistency with which project performance is measured. Just as the sage does not differentiate between individuals based on their external characteristics, performance should be evaluated consistently across all project tasks, roles and phases. This ensures that no individual or team member is unfairly judged, and it provides a clear and continuous picture of the project's overall progress.

Consistent performance evaluation also helps in identifying trends, which can be used to assess the project's health over time. It provides a reliable basis for comparison, making it easier to identify issues early on and take corrective action before problems escalate. Furthermore, a consistent evaluation process can highlight best practices that can be replicated or refined to improve the overall efficiency of the project.

- **Encouraging Continuous Improvement**

Krishna's teachings also inspire continuous improvement—another crucial aspect of performance measurement. By measuring performance in an objective, unbiased manner, project managers are better equipped to spot gaps and areas that need improvement. This continuous cycle of measuring, assessing and acting based on clear, impartial data empowers teams to make iterative improvements throughout the project.

For instance, if certain tasks are consistently behind schedule or over budget, these discrepancies can be identified early through regular performance reviews. Project managers can then implement corrective measures, providing the team with a roadmap for better performance in the future. Krishna's philosophy encourages this ongoing learning process, where each cycle of performance assessment contributes to both the individual and project's growth.

By keeping performance measurements clear, consistent and impartial, project managers not only ensure a fair evaluation process but also pave the way for ongoing success and continuous improvement throughout the project's lifecycle.

In this way, Krishna's wisdom provides a powerful framework for approaching project measurement. By embracing fairness, objectivity and consistency, project managers can ensure that all aspects of performance are evaluated impartially and transparently, creating a strong foundation for effective decision-making and long-term project success.

8. **Uncertainty Performance**

    - ***Verse:*** *'Anityam asukham lokam, imam prapya bhajasva mam'* (9.33)
    - ***Meaning:*** 'This world is temporary and full of suffering; engage in my devotion.'
    - ***Connection:*** Uncertainty is an inherent part of both life and project management. Krishna's recognition of the transient and unpredictable nature of life aligns deeply with the **Uncertainty Performance** domain in project management. Whether we are facing **known-known risks**—those that can be anticipated and planned for—or **unknown-unknown risks**—those that arise unexpectedly—Krishna's teachings offer valuable insights on how to manage uncertainty effectively.

In project management, uncertainty can emerge in many forms. There are risks that can be predicted, such as potential resource shortages or project delays, and then there are those risks that cannot be foreseen, like market disruptions, sudden changes in regulations or unforeseen technical failures. Krishna teaches us that the key to dealing with uncertainty is not to resist it but to accept it and respond with resilience and focus, staying committed to our purpose despite the challenges that may arise. This principle is vital when managing the uncertainties inherent in projects.

- **Understanding Uncertainty Performance in PMBOK**

According to the **PMBOK Guide**, **Uncertainty Performance** is all about how project teams identify, assess and respond to risks throughout the project lifecycle. It involves both managing **predictable risks** and adapting to **unforeseen challenges** that may emerge unexpectedly. The project manager must proactively identify and assess risks, develop risk management plans and then monitor these risks as the project progresses, adapting the plan as necessary.

In practical terms, managing uncertainty involves two main strategies: preparation and adaptability. By embracing both **known-known** and **unknown-unknown risks**, project managers can ensure that the project team remains focused, flexible and ready to respond when things don't go according to plan.

- **Handling Uncertainty**

Known-Known Risks: These are risks that are foreseeable and can be planned for. Examples include known delays due to resource unavailability or equipment malfunction. Project managers can anticipate these risks early, assess their potential impact and develop mitigation strategies accordingly. For instance, creating contingency plans, allocating extra time for known delays or having backup resources in place can help address these risks before they affect the project.

Unknown-Unknown Risks: These are the unpredictable risks that emerge without warning, like a sudden regulatory change or an unforeseen market shift. These types of risks are challenging because they cannot be planned in advance. However, Krishna's teachings encourage us to remain resilient and focused on the larger goal, even in the face of such unexpected challenges. The key is to build flexibility into the project plan, creating space for quick adaptation when unforeseen risks occur. By maintaining a mindset of adaptability and openness to change, project teams can better respond to these unknowns as they arise.

- **Documenting Uncertainty**

An essential part of managing uncertainty in project management is proper documentation. The **risk register** should be used to document known risks along with their likelihood, impact and mitigation strategies. For **unknown-unknown risks**, while we can't predict them, we can prepare for them by creating a contingency plan or 'buffer' in the project timeline or budget. Throughout the project, the risk register should be regularly updated as new risks emerge, ensuring that the team is aware of and ready to address new uncertainties.

The act of documenting uncertainty is not just about tracking risks, but also about fostering a culture of proactive thinking. It allows the team to anticipate potential challenges, learn from unforeseen issues and refine their risk management practices over time. This iterative process of documentation and reflection helps in mitigating future uncertainties.

- **Mitigating Uncertainty**

Mitigating uncertainty involves both planned responses to known risks and developing strategies to address unexpected challenges. For **known-known risks**, project managers can implement mitigation measures that have been developed during the planning phase. These may include allocating extra resources, adjusting timelines or negotiating with vendors.

For **unknown-unknown risks**, the approach is more about building resilience. Creating a flexible project plan that allows room for adjustments, having open lines of communication within the team and encouraging adaptability are all essential for navigating the unforeseen. This approach aligns with Krishna's teachings on resilience and devotion to the process, regardless of the results. The team must remain committed to the project's purpose and goals, regardless of the uncertainties they face along the way.

Additional Verses for Uncertainty Performance

Verse: *'Dukheshu anudvigna-manah, sukheshu vigata-sprihah'* (2.14)
Meaning: 'The wise person, whose mind is undisturbed by sorrow and who is free from desire in happiness, is said to be in a state of yoga.'

This verse offers an important lesson in managing uncertainty. Krishna teaches us that we must remain undisturbed by sorrow and unattached to joy, which is a key mindset for managing uncertainty in projects. When known risks emerge, project managers who are undisturbed can stay focused on the task at hand, managing the situation with a calm and composed mind.

Similarly, when unexpected challenges arise, this equanimity allows for clear thinking and effective decision-making.

Verse: *'Karmanye vadhikaraste, ma phaleshu kadachana'* (2.47) **Meaning:** 'You have the right to perform your prescribed duties, but you are not entitled to the fruits of your actions.'

This verse speaks to the importance of focusing on the process rather than becoming attached to the outcome. In project management, uncertainty often means that the outcome is beyond our control. By focusing on managing the project well—executing tasks, mitigating risks and adapting to unforeseen challenges—we fulfill our duties, regardless of what the final results may be. This approach helps reduce stress and allows project teams to remain focused on what they can control, without becoming overwhelmed by uncertainty.

- **Conclusion: Cultivating Resilience and Focus**

Krishna's teachings provide profound insights into navigating uncertainty, which are especially relevant for project managers. By embracing both **known-known** and **unknown-unknown risks** with resilience and adaptability, project teams can remain focused on the greater purpose of the project. Krishna's wisdom teaches us not to resist uncertainty, but to accept it as an inevitable part of the journey. Through careful documentation, proactive mitigation and a mindset of equanimity, project managers can successfully navigate the unpredictable landscape of project risks, ensuring that the team stays on course even when faced with challenges beyond their control. By continuously learning and adapting, project teams can handle uncertainty more effectively, ensuring the project's ultimate success despite the unpredictability that lies ahead.

Doing Right vs. Getting It Done: A Leadership Challenge and Paradox

When I first started reading the ***Shrimad Bhagavad Gita,*** I was searching for guidance to address the complex challenges of my professional life. At that point, I had spent years in project and programme management, handling multi-layered teams, coordinating enterprise-level initiatives and navigating situations where timelines, budgets and stakeholder expectations often seemed impossible to balance. My mindset was deeply shaped by frameworks like **PMBOK**, where success is measured in terms of deliverables, milestones and outcomes. Every project had defined objectives, clear metrics for achievement and a structured process to monitor performance. To me, managing projects meant ensuring that the goals were met efficiently and effectively.

As I immersed myself in the *Shrimad Bhagavad Gita,* I encountered teachings that at first seemed almost contradictory to my experience. Krishna's central message to Arjun emphasised ***karma yoga,*** the performance of one's duty without attachment to outcomes. He repeatedly urged **Arjun** to focus on **acting rightly**, guided by *dharma,* ethics and intention, rather than worrying about victory, loss or personal gain. I found myself puzzled. How could a text so revered offer guidance for someone like me, whose daily work revolves around achieving measurable results? I began to question: *If results are not the ultimate priority, how can one gauge success? How does one make decisions when deliverables are on the line?*

This initial confusion stayed with me. I wrestled with the apparent paradox: on one hand, **PMBOK and modern project management frameworks** focus heavily on outcomes, benefits realisation and performance metrics. On the other hand, Krishna's philosophy emphasises detached action, the righteousness of the process itself and the alignment of one's efforts with a larger purpose. At first glance, it seemed that these two approaches could not coexist—the professional world demands tangible results, yet the *Gita* asks us to release attachment to them.

It took **multiple readings of the *Shrimad Bhagavad Gita*,** long reflections and conversations with my parents, mentors and elders to recognise the truth: what initially seemed like a contradiction was, in fact, a profound **complementarity**. The tension between 'doing right' and 'getting it done' is not a flaw; it is the very space where effective leadership and project management emerge. Krishna's teachings do not dismiss outcomes—they enrich them by ensuring that the path to success is guided by ethics, integrity and clarity of purpose.

From this perspective, the PMBOK and *karma yoga* address different dimensions of the same challenge. The PMBOK provides the **structural tools** for managing projects: defining scope, managing risks, controlling costs, tracking schedules, engaging stakeholders and ensuring quality. It answers the 'how' and 'what' of project delivery. Krishna's teachings address the **inner framework** of the project manager: the mindset, the ethical compass, the emotional resilience and the focus on righteous action. It answers the 'why' and 'with what intention' of every decision and action.

Once I began to reconcile these perspectives, the synergy became clear. In practice, this integration transforms leadership and project execution in several ways:

1. **Focused Action Meets Structured Execution**

Krishna's guidance encourages us to immerse ourselves fully in our duties, with diligence and clarity. When applied to a modern project, this complements structured the PMBOK processes. Planning, monitoring and executing tasks are done with discipline, while being performed with intention and care, rather than under the constant stress of attachment to outcomes. This approach ensures that the project progresses efficiently, yet with a mindfulness that elevates the quality of decisions and team engagement.

2. **Ethics Enhance Performance**

Modern frameworks stress governance and stakeholder engagement, but often the focus is on efficiency and risk mitigation. Krishna's teachings remind us that **how we act matters as much as what we achieve.** Decisions rooted in ethics, fairness and integrity reduce long-term conflicts, foster trust and ensure that the results of a project are respected, sustainable and meaningful. When leaders act ethically, outcomes are more reliable and teams are more aligned and motivated.

3. **Resilience Under Uncertainty**

Projects rarely unfold exactly as planned. PMBOK offers tools for risk management, but the *Gita* instils mental resilience and emotional intelligence. By practising *karma yoga,* I have learned to navigate uncertainty with calm and focus. Even when timelines slip, stakeholders change priorities or unforeseen issues arise, acting with clarity and detachment allows for measured responses, creativity in problem-solving and steady leadership.

4. **Long-Term Alignment**

Karma yoga emphasises acting in alignment with a larger purpose, beyond short-term results. In project management, this mirrors the PMBOK principle of benefits realisation and strategic alignment. When a leader is anchored in purpose, decisions are made with the long-term vision in mind, ensuring that actions contribute not just to immediate project objectives but to broader organisational goals and values.

5. **Sustainable High Performance**

Acting rightly, with focus on duty rather than attachment to immediate outcomes, naturally leads to sustainable performance. When teams see leaders who are principled, steady and aligned with purpose, they are more likely to be committed, collaborative and resilient. Decisions made under pressure but grounded in ethical action often result in solutions that are robust and enduring.

Throughout my professional journey, this integration has been transformative. I recall handling projects with multiple moving parts, tight deadlines and high stakes. Initially, my natural inclination was to fixate on results, to chase deliverables and to control every aspect of the outcome. But by consciously applying Krishna's teachings, I began to approach challenges differently. I focused on **doing the right things, acting with integrity and guiding my teams with clarity**, while using structured project management processes to organise work and track progress. The result was not only **successful project outcomes** but also **stronger teams, better collaboration and decisions that I could stand by with pride**.

In essence, what appeared as a paradox—the PMBOK's outcome-driven approach versus Krishna's focus on duty—reveals itself as a **powerful duality**. Outcomes and ethical action are not mutually exclusive; they are mutually reinforcing. Structured project management ensures that objectives are met, while *karma yoga* ensures that the path to achieving them is principled, focused and resilient. Together, they create a **leadership model that is both effective and enduring**.

This realisation changed how I lead, make decisions and mentor others. It encouraged me to consider not just whether a project succeeds, but how it succeeds. Are actions aligned with principles? Are stakeholders treated fairly? Is the team empowered and motivated? Are challenges addressed with clarity, resilience and foresight? When these questions guide action, outcomes naturally follow and the value created is far greater than mere deliverables.

Reading the *Shrimad Bhagavad Gita* repeatedly, reflecting on its teachings and discussing its wisdom with mentors and elders helped me internalise this dual approach. I learned to embrace the paradox, understanding that **great leadership is not only about getting it done but also about doing it rightly**. This balance between results and ethics, execution and intention, strategy and values, has become a cornerstone of how I lead teams, manage projects and approach life itself.

In conclusion, the apparent conflict between the PMBOK's outcome orientation and Krishna's *karma*-centred philosophy is not a limitation—it is a **lesson integrated in leadership**. By combining structured, results-focused project management with action rooted in ethics, duty and clarity, we achieve a more holistic, sustainable and inspiring approach to leadership. The journey from initial confusion to deep understanding mirrors the path of any professional striving to lead with both **effectiveness and integrity**, proving that in the intersection of doing right and getting it done lies the essence of true leadership.

Conclusion: Timeless Lessons from the Divine Project Manager

As we come to the close of this exploration, one truth becomes abundantly clear: Lord Krishna was not just a spiritual guide and philosopher; he was an unparalleled M=master of project management. Through the events of the *Mahabharata,* Krishna exemplified skills that modern organisations spend millions trying to teach their leaders—strategic planning, stakeholder management, risk mitigation, conflict resolution and resource optimisation. His genius lay not only in understanding the mechanics of success but in aligning them with a higher purpose, ethics and human values.

Krishna's approach reminds us that project management is far more than processes, tools or charts. It is the art of understanding people, anticipating challenges and orchestrating diverse talents towards a common goal. From his careful guidance of Arjun on the battlefield to the subtle manoeuvres that ensured the Pandavas' victory, Krishna consistently demonstrated a blend of foresight, adaptability and ethical clarity. He managed not only tasks and timelines but the hearts and minds of his stakeholders. In every challenge, whether mundane or monumental, he exhibited a rare balance between strategy and empathy, control and flexibility.

Modern project managers can draw immense inspiration from Krishna's methods. His life teaches us that success lies not merely in completing deliverables but in creating harmony among teams, maintaining transparency and fostering trust. The emphasis on foresight—preparing for every eventuality without succumbing to panic—is as relevant today as it was in ancient times. His subtle risk management, problem-solving skills and conflict resolution strategies show that a leader's effectiveness is measured as much by how they navigate human complexities as by how they execute tasks.

Furthermore, Krishna's mastery of the 'triple constraints'—cost, time and quality—was never mechanical. He understood that every decision has cascading effects, and the best managers are those who can balance multiple priorities without compromising the greater purpose. His examples illustrate that true leadership transcends authority; it manifests in influence, persuasion and inspiring people to rise above their limitations.

Beyond the tangible lessons of project management, Krishna also imparts a deeper principle: the importance of vision. A project without a clear vision may succeed temporarily, but it will falter in the long run. Krishna's clarity of purpose, combined with a deep understanding of his team's strengths and weaknesses, ensured outcomes that were sustainable, ethical and transformational.

In reflecting upon Krishna as the ultimate project manager, one realises that the tools and techniques of modern project management—while valuable—are only truly effective when coupled with wisdom, foresight and humanity. His life demonstrates that leadership is not about imposing control; it is about nurturing trust, creating alignment and guiding people to achieve goals that surpass individual ambitions.

As you close this book, take a moment to internalise these lessons. Whether you lead a multinational project, manage a small team or even navigate your personal goals, Krishna's example is a beacon. By embracing strategic thinking, empathy, adaptability and ethical decision-making, you too can elevate your management practice to a level that is not just successful, but exemplary.

In conclusion, Lord Krishna remains the archetype of the perfect project manager—not merely because he achieved victories, but because he demonstrated how greatness is born from vision, balance and unwavering commitment to a higher purpose. His life challenges us to rethink our approach to leadership and project management: to infuse our work with clarity, integrity and care for those we lead. In doing so, every project, no matter how complex, becomes not just a task to complete but an opportunity to create a meaningful, lasting impact.

May the lessons of Krishna inspire us all to lead with wisdom, manage with skill and achieve with purpose. The path he illuminates is timeless, guiding not just the completion of projects, but the creation of enduring value in the world around us.

Author Biography – Pankaj Balooni

Hi, I'm Pankaj Balooni—an amateur poet and writer who finds joy in storytelling. While my professional journey spans nearly two decades in IT project management, my heart has always been drawn to the beauty of words. Writing allows me to capture emotions, reflect on life's experiences and express thoughts that might otherwise go unspoken.

Since childhood, I have been fascinated by the power of stories—how they can transport us to different worlds, challenge our thinking and leave a lasting impression. Over the years, I found myself drawn to writing, not just as a creative outlet but as a way to document experiences, ideas and emotions that shape our lives. Whether through poetry, short reflections or full-length stories, I believe in the magic of words and their ability to connect people across cultures, backgrounds and perspectives.

I took my first step into publishing with *'Shreyash and a Tooth Fairy,'* a book I released on Amazon KDP. The story was inspired by a real-life moment with my son, Shreyash. Like many parents, when one of his wobbling baby teeth finally came out, my wife and I placed a coin under his pillow, ensuring he woke up believing the tooth fairy had visited him. It was a small tradition, but witnessing his excitement in the morning made me think about how such little gestures create lasting childhood memories. That experience stayed with me, compelling me to turn it into a story for other children and parents to enjoy.

However, beyond being a simple children's book, *'Shreyash and a Tooth Fairy'* also touches on some thought-provoking concepts. The story briefly explores different dimensions of the universe—2D, 3D, 4D, 5D, and beyond—where celestial bodies can travel. I wanted to introduce young minds to the wonders of space and time in a fun and engaging way, encouraging curiosity about the mysteries that exist beyond what we see. My goal was to spark a sense of wonder and encourage readers, both young and old, to think beyond the limits of their everyday experiences.

In addition to my passion for writing, I am also the founder of **GIT Software Technologies Ltd.**, a UK-based IT company. My journey in the corporate world has been driven by a vision to create innovative business solutions while fostering a workplace culture that values its people as much as its goals. Over the years, I have worked with diverse teams across different industries, helping businesses streamline their operations and embrace technological advancements. I strongly believe that success is not just about financial growth but about creating an environment where people feel empowered, motivated and inspired to contribute their best.

Beyond my professional and literary pursuits, I have always been deeply fascinated by religious texts from various faiths. I love reading them not just for their spiritual wisdom but for their profound insights into humanity, morality and life's deeper meaning. I often reflect on how these teachings align with real-life situations—what lessons can truly be implemented in today's world and which ones remain idealistic concepts.

This ongoing exploration has shaped my perspective on life, relationships and the human experience. It has also influenced my writing, as I often find myself weaving these reflections into my stories and poetry.

For me, writing is more than just putting words on paper; it is a way to express thoughts that might otherwise remain unspoken. It is a way to connect with people, share experiences and spark meaningful conversations. Every story has the potential to inspire, to heal and to challenge the way we see the world.

When I'm not working, writing or reading, I enjoy spending time with my family, engaging in deep conversations about life and exploring new perspectives through books and travel.

With this manuscript, I take another step towards sharing my thoughts and stories with a wider audience. I hope my words resonate with readers, encourage curiosity and perhaps even offer new perspectives on the world around us.

Warm Regards,

Pankaj Balooni